CONCEPT BOOKS · 9

CHILD DEVELOPMENT

CONCEPT BOOKS

General Editor: Alan Harris

CHILD DEVELOPMENT

NORMAN WILLIAMS

Research Fellow in Psychology,
Farmington Trust Research Unit

 HEINEMANN EDUCATIONAL BOOKS

LONDON

Heinemann Educational Books Ltd
LONDON EDINBURGH MELBOURNE AUCKLAND TORONTO
SINGAPORE HONG KONG KUALA LUMPUR
NAIROBI IBADAN JOHANNESBURG
LUSAKA NEW DELHI

ISBN 0 435 46188 5

Published in Great Britain by
Heinemann Educational Books Ltd
48 Charles Street, London W1X 8AH
Printed Offset Litho and bound by
Cox & Wyman Ltd, London, Fakenham and Reading

Contents

Acknowledgement

Figure 6 on page 39 is reproduced from *Human Anatomy* by Morris with the permission of McGraw-Hill Book Company.

Figure 10 on page 50 is reproduced from *Mankind Evolving* by T. Dobzansky with the permission of the Yale University Press.

Introduction

ANOTHER book on child development? The overcrowded library shelves are already creaking under the weight of the bewildering miscellany of large and small books on this topic. Can there be any justification in adding to them, except when the new book is describing some important new advance in our knowledge of the subject?

The justification is to be found partly in the general aim of the series. There is a large number of readers, many of them in, or having recently left, the sixth forms, who want a short introduction to the basic concepts employed in a wide array of subjects not taught in the schools. We have heard a great deal in recent years about the 'explosion of knowledge' and the accompanying 'explosion of literature', but it is not always fully appreciated what these entail for the reader. These descriptions do not refer just to the multiplication of disciplines and fields of study; within any single topic there is an increasing diversification of points of view and of methods of study and research. It is not simply that there is *more* knowledge on a given subject, in the sense of a greater accumulation of the same *kind* of fact; it is rather that we are faced with new *kinds* of knowledge – different ways of approaching perhaps familiar topics, new dimensions of insight arising from new techniques.

It might be supposed that purely descriptive subjects might not conform to this trend; that descriptive zoology, say, can not expand at the same rate since there is a steadily decreasing number of species of organism left unclassified (at any rate, until space research makes a further dramatic advance). Whether or not it is true of such sciences, this certainly does not apply to the study of child development, which must always be more than simply a descriptive or classificatory study. The author inevitably provides some sort of interpretation of the data. There is always a *theory* of development. Even in his choice of a method of gathering facts – experiment, observation, interview and so on – an author is giving a certain slant to his work, and the methods available are as varied in this field as in others. The study of child development is no exception to the general trend towards greater complexity.

Paradoxically, then, the justification for adding to the already large child development literature lies in part in its very range and diversity. We are coming to the point where a preliminary orientation is essential. Consider, for instance, the following half-dozen examples, all very much condensed, but representative of what you might meet in a number of books on the subject.

(a) Let us begin by looking at the work of a research institute which is concerned with child development. A typical scene contains three characters – a research worker is talking to a pre-school child while an observer sits at the other side of the room, taking notes on what happens. The experimenter has a number of jars of different shapes. He pours some water into a short wide jar and then lets the child pour it into another one, which is tall and narrow. Naturally, the level of the water in the second jar is much higher.

'Is there more water than there was before? Or less?' the experimenter asks.

'More,' the child says confidently.

The work continues along these lines, with the experimenter exploring the child's perception of volume by apparently simple questions.

Other topics are examined with similarly simple equipment, or with no equipment at all, as in the following example, which shows very clearly how these extremely simple questions can be very illuminating.

'Have you got a sister?' the experimenter asks a little girl.
'Yes.'
'What is her name?'
'Mary.'
'And has Mary got a sister?'
'No.'

(b) Let us now look at an experiment of a different kind. It was carried out over thirty years ago, but it is still reported in a number of textbooks on child development.

This experimenter was interested in the part played by simple experiences in the first few months of life on the development of the child. In particular, he wished to discover whether environmental stimulation promotes development, and conversely whether its absence retards the child. By 'environmental stimulation' he is referring simply to the sum total of impressions the child receives from the outside world by means of his sense organs, whether these impressions arise from people picking him up and cuddling him or speaking to him, or whether they are simply the random sights and sounds and smells which impinge on his senses in a normal noisy family.

Our experimenter reared two infants under conditions of 'minimal environmental stimulation'. That is, the children were not handled or nursed or spoken to apart from what was necessary to keep them fed and clean and physically comfortable. The experiment was discontinued when the infants were about seven months old and the experimenter compared the level of development of his two small subjects with the norms for children of a similar age. He came to the conclusion that his subjects did not differ significantly from infants of a similar age who had not been raised in this restricted way. A great many of the actions which we carry out when bringing up children, he reasoned, are thus shown to be unnecessary and superfluous.

However, I can now quote another experiment on the same topic, a recent one, which is not yet in any of the textbooks on the subject. On this occasion twenty infants between five and six

months were allocated at random to two groups, an experimental
group and a control group.

All the infants were given standard tests, which expressed the
child's level of development in the form of a figure called a
'developmental quotient' (discussed in more detail below, p. 58).
Children in both groups were given the same test on three successive days, but the treatment of the two groups differed for the
twelve minutes immediately before the test.

Let us consider the experimental group first. Immediately
before the first test, they were given a twelve minute 'period of
non-stimulation' during which time the child was left without toys
in a quiet room, his field of vision being restricted by means of
screens placed round his cot. The treatment was changed, however, before the second and third tests. For these, the experimenters substituted a 'stimulation period' of the same duration,
when, for twelve minutes, someone would talk to the child, smile
at him, pick him up and fondle him. The control group, on the
other hand, had the twelve minute non-stimulation period before
each of the tests.

The argument behind the structure of this experiment was, of
course, that differences in the test results of the two groups of
children could be ascribed to the differences in their treatment,
and that they would therefore reflect the influence of environmental stimulation.

The test results in fact showed that, while the developmental
quotients of the control group were unchanged, those of the experimental group rose after the change from non-stimulation to
stimulation. The experimenters concluded, from this evidence,
that environmental stimulation does indeed play an important
part in the development of the child.

Let us turn from accounts of experimental work to straight
statements about the child's development.
(c) One book tells us that the sixth year (to open the book at
random) brings fundamental changes to the child. On the physical
level, he is losing his milk teeth and undergoing changes of body

chemistry which make him more susceptible to infectious diseases. Psychologically, he tends to show wild swings between diametrically opposite forms of behaviour – his crying is easily diverted into laughter, and vice versa. He is beginning to take an active interest in reading and will often pretend to read his favourite stories for himself, remembering the words from when some adult has read the story to him, and turning the pages as though he were actually following the printed letters. He is able to recognize a few single words, and even picks them out sometimes from unfamiliar settings, such as his parents' magazines.

(d) Taking another book from the shelf, we find a paediatrician talking about the emotional relationship which exists between a mother and her baby. If this is developing naturally, he argues, then there is no need for special feeding techniques and weighing and measurement and tables of norms. The infant takes the right amount of milk at the right speed and knows when to stop. The physical process works so well because of the existence of this naturally developing emotional relationship between mother and child, in which they both take pleasure. The real trouble, he tells us, is that mothers too easily fall a prey to the advice of puritans, who feel that sensations of pleasure of this kind must be wrong.

(e) Opening another child development book at the chapter dealing with adolescence, we read an account of how the pituitary gland stimulates the development of the sex glands. These begin to secrete their own specific hormones in the bloodstream, and this in turn brings about the changes which we associate with the onset of sexual maturity. These are of two kinds. First, we have those which are directly concerned with the reproductive process. At the same time, they produce the secondary sexual characteristics, such as the appearance of facial hair and a deeper voice in boys, and the development of breasts in girls.

(f) Our final example is one which is referred to in very many child development books and is concerned with the famous Oedipus complex. This theory is that the young boy's sexual interests focus on his mother and that he has in his mind the idea of replacing his father. Usually, of course, this is rejected by both parents. The central features of the resulting situation are the child's feeling of hostility and rivalry towards his father. The child cannot cope with the tension and fear involved, and so he eventually represses this sexual ambition and identifies with his father. This solution is crucial for the later development of the boy's character.

The range of examples could be expanded even further, but the six given are sufficient to illustrate a number of points, which underline the need for some orientation for the newcomer to the subject.

In the first place not all child development books have the same aim; there are, for instance, what we might call persuasive, as opposed to explanatory aims. Books of this kind are written to persuade the reader of the rightness of a particular view rather than to give a straight account of some aspect of the development process. Persuasive writing of this kind frequently embodies assumptions about the value of certain things, and such judgements may be quite subjective. The paediatrician, for instance, in the fourth example is writing for a particular audience, and is attempting to bring about changes in the attitudes of young mothers. To do this, he refers to the effects of Puritanism, and this part of his statement, at least, is clearly the expression of his personal opinion. That is not to say that it is wrong, but that it has an entirely different status from statements like those concerning stimulation in the first example.

This brings us to a further distinction, between accounts which are objective descriptions of the outcome of observation and experiment, and those which involve subjective value judgements. These latter cases are something we must always watch out for. Our paediatrician was quite open about what he was doing. No one could mistake his statement for anything but a forceful way of expressing his opinion based on his own observations. Unfortunately it is not always as clear as this. As we shall see in a later chapter, it is all too easy for value judgements to be concealed in what appear to be quite objective statements of the development process. This is something we need to be aware of when approaching books of this kind.

We make a further distinction between general and specific studies. Is the author trying to give us an overall picture of the development of the child, or is he concerned with the growth of some particular attribute? In the examples given above, we find one which is concerned with the child's intellectual development in a fairly narrow sense, and another concerned with a specific range of physiological phenomena. These may be contrasted with the account which lists a very large number of different norms for a particular age group.

There are also clear differences in method. On the one hand, we have information which is based on approaches which we can roughly describe as 'experimental', and on the other those which are based on less formal observations. How is the general reader to evaluate these two approaches? There are difficulties even within one approach. The first two examples are both based on experimental procedures, but it can be seen at once that there are marked differences in the way the experimenter sets about his task. And what of the two experiments which were concerned with sensory stimulation? Each of them may seem 'scientific' to the reader who has not had a training in the social sciences, but, as we have seen, they appear to point to opposite conclusions. Were there experimental errors made in one case? And is one of these experiments therefore more valid than the other? If the experts cannot agree, how is the layman to distinguish between various approaches, let alone to fit them together into a picture of the whole child?

It is of course impossible to answer all of these questions in a book of this size. It is equally impossible to give a complete rounded account of the processes of child development from birth to maturity. Instead, what is planned is an introductory book, which it is hoped, will provide a key which will enable the newcomer to approach more detailed or more technical books on the subject and to find his way through this burgeoning section of psychological literature.

The plan of the book is quite simple. In Part One, we shall look at some of the basic concepts employed in child development studies to see exactly what they mean. We shall then move on to look in Part Two at a few theories of child development which have been chosen to show how these concepts may be strung together in practice to provide quite different models.

You have already seen that, in this topic, there is no unanimity among authors as regards the proper approach, and, sometimes even, the correct conclusions. For the most part, the intention is that this book will be neutral as between various theoretical approaches, while pointing out some of their limitations and difficulties. That is not to say, however, that the book does not contain a point of view of its own. The view implicit in what follows is that any theories of child development should be viewed simply as models, which are constructed to help us understand what is going on and to predict what is likely to happen next. They should *not* be regarded as ideas which are 'true' in any absolute sense. The criterion must be whether they are useful. Such theories are, rather, tools, and as with hammers and spanners and tools of that kind, each of them may be entirely appropriate for different purposes.

Finally, I will point out before the reader discovers it for himself that this book is an apparent anomaly – a book on child development which does not present an account of how a child develops. The reason for this is implied by what has already been said. There exist already very many books which do this job. The aim of the present one is to enable you to read them more easily and with greater insight.

PART ONE

one

Methods of Child Study

A GOOD deal depends on the method used to gather data on child development. All writing on the subject should have its basis in some form of observation or study of real children, but unfortunately that is not always the case. Many theories of development are based more on ideological assumptions than with any consideration of what children are really like. We usually associate this kind of bias with extreme political positions, but this is not the only situation in which it can be seen. A discussion of the child's moral development in terms of 'original sin' may take the theological concept rather than the child's behaviour as its starting-point. And this is in fact the first question we should ask ourselves about any theory of child development: is the writer constructing a theory in order to make sense of what he has seen children do, or is he looking for aspects of behaviour which provide illustrations for a theory which already exists?

Even some well-known and respected discussions of children may suffer from this lack of objectivity. Most students of education read at some time or other *Emile*, a description by the eighteenth-century French writer, Rousseau, of a boy's education. It is based on Rousseau's idea of what constituted a good and natural education. Rousseau was very impressed by the idea of the 'noble savage', a natural man, untainted by the vices of civilization, and used him as an exemplar in planning a 'natural education'. Unfortunately, whatever its merits in other directions, the book seems to have been written in ignorance of what children and, for that matter, 'savages' are really like. I am not arguing that such books are worthless, but that if they have any value, it is not as sources of data on how children develop.

But even if we leave aside this section of the literature and concentrate on those studies which are child based, we still find that the choice of method is important. As I suggested in the introduction, there is a wide variety of approaches to our subject. To some extent the *method* of study chosen will affect the *kind* of data produced by a particular study, and also to a still greater degree it will affect the weight we attach to its findings. A survey of 1,000 eight-year-olds differs from an intensive study of the development of one child over a period of, say, five years, not merely in terms of numbers, but in the *kind* of data obtained. That is not to say that one of these methods is 'good', and the other 'bad', but simply that each gives a different perspective, that the strength of each lies in a different (and complementary) direction. (Though, of course, we would generally attach greater importance to findings based on rigorously methodical observation of children than to those which depend on generalizations resting on a few chance encounters.)

In this chapter, therefore, I shall discuss some of the possible approaches to the subject, and examine some of their uses and limitations.

The most familiar basis for comments and statements about children is, of course, informal observation by parents, teachers and others who have contact with children. It is the method which has been with us for the thousands of years before the advent of psychologically based developmental studies. We should not be inclined to dismiss it out of hand on account of its informality. Often it is extremely accurate. A mother who has brought up several children, may say of a neighbour's child, 'He should have started to talk three months ago. You ought to get a doctor to see that he's all right'. Although statements of this kind are intuitively rather than statistically based, they can be (as in this case) extremely helpful and accurate.

Of course, as a method of collecting data, it has obvious limitations. In the first place, people who, like parents, have a close relationship with the subject of the observations, are not always entirely accurate in their reporting. I do not mean that they are deliberately telling lies. But the average doting parent has, emotionally speaking, a vested interest in putting the best possible interpretation on the facts, even if this means that the facts have to be slightly distorted. Parents usually want to feel that their child is clever, or strong, or skilful. The child is, in a way, an extension of themselves, and we know how difficult it is to be honest about ourselves. You may have heard people arguing about whether the smiling expression we sometimes see on a baby's face is indeed a smile, or merely a reaction to some internal state of affairs, like indigestion or wind. (This is not so trivial a point as you may suppose, since, if the baby is really smiling at his mother, it indicates that he is capable of distinguishing her from other people and responding to her presence – important early steps in his perceptual and social development.) You may have noticed that it is commonly the case in such arguments that it is the mother who insists that it is a genuine smile, and some emotionally detached iconoclast who takes the opposite view. The point is, of course, that the mother is very proud of her new baby; she wants him to be intelligent and to recognize her. She also loves the baby; it makes her feel good if he smiles at her. If we want an *objective* statement about what the baby is doing, the mother is the last person we would go to – her actual perception of what is going on is coloured by what she *wants* to be the case. In fact, you will find from books on child development that the mother's interpretation of the facts is probably right, but we base this on other observations, and not merely on her opinion.

This sort of prejudice may intrude on observations even when there is no personal involvement with their object. I can remember hearing two teachers from a secondary modern school describing the same class of children. Neither teacher seemed to have had any real disciplinary problems, but their accounts were very different. According to one description, they were aggressively delinquent, always looking for trouble, and only held in check by the teacher's unusual toughness and skill; according to the other, the children were helpful and considerate, and always eager to learn. Although it is quite possible that the two teachers did have significantly different experiences with the class, it was also plain to anyone who knew them that the descriptions were distorted (unconsciously, we hope) to promote a particular image of themselves which was important to them.

A weakness, then, of informal observation as a sole method of finding out about children is that its informality leaves uncontrolled so many factors that irrelevant matters, such as emotional need, personality – or even the fashion in opinions – can distort the way the events are perceived. Another way of putting this is to say that it is very difficult to separate observation from interpretation of what is seen, when using this sort of data. This is a point which is well understood in a number of activities – in newspaper reporting, for instance, where great importance is attached to the distinction between news and editorial opinions – but is is not always applied to our present field.

Of course, there may be actual, as opposed to merely perceived differences in the object of the observations. A man who has been a public school housemaster for twenty years may have a very different experience of the development of adolescent boys from that of a housemaster in an approved school.

We can go some way towards overcoming the unreliability of these methods by attempting to standardize our observations. One way to do this is to make more formal, or manipulate, the situation in which they are carried out. This brings us to the next group of methods.

Suppose that we wish to establish the date at which a baby learns to walk or a schoolboy is capable of understanding algebraic concepts. As we have seen, one way of doing this is to gather the observations of people who happen to have been in contact with children while they were doing these things. But we have argued that this may be distorted by the intrusion of the observer's opinions or prejudices, or confused by implicit interpretations; or the children he dealt with may be atypical in some way.

So we may carry out, instead, tests of several thousand children, and find out from the results what is the average point at which these events occur. The most obvious difference between such a procedure and informal observations is that the numbers concerned are very much larger, but this may not in fact be the most important difference. What is important is that we are creating a standardized situation in which it is possible to make the necessary observations in a methodical and formalized way. Thus, we may regard a number of other methods of investigation as falling under this heading. Interviews, for example, when they are designed to find out whether the child has formed certain concepts, are essentially the same process of creating a particular situation in which we can make our observations. Most tests of intelligence, or of attainment in various fields, follow the same pattern. So, too, are the 'structured observations' described in the example in the introduction in which the child is working out problems with jars of water.

Methods of this sort are very widely used to establish norms and developmental sequences. They can tell us a great deal about the rate of growth of a child's vocabulary, about the pattern of personality development, or about the emergence of social attitudes. Their limitation, however, lies in the fact that they are not so well able to provide data about *causal* processes. The following example will show what I mean. If we are interested in the development of children's vocabulary, it is not too difficult a matter to construct a vocabulary test and give this to a very large number of children of different ages. Two different conclusions would be likely to emerge from such a survey. Firstly, we would have an overall pattern of growth, represented by the number of words known accurately by children of different ages. (Such a table is in fact given below in a subsequent chapter.) Secondly, we would find that there would be wide differences in the performance of individual children. This might be due to a number of factors. The most obvious one is intelligence, but it has recently been suggested that a large part of such differences is due to the effect of social class. We would be able to provide some sort of answer as to which of these factors is responsible by analysing the results of our survey. Provided that we had the relevant data available, we could compare intelligent children with unintelligent children, and members of higher with members of lower social classes. What we could not be sure about, however, would be that the sample of children we selected was not such that some other important causal factor might be operating, about which we know nothing. Of course, we can formalize our survey still further, so that we are dealing with different groups of children who are identical, except as regards the factor we are investigating, but this leads us to a more sophisticated type of study which will be dealt with presently.[1]

The methods discussed so far have been based on *observations* of particular achievements or aspects of development, and we have seen that they can be more formalized by constructing an artificial environment. To overcome their weakness in accounting for causal influences, it is possible to use an entirely different method. This is the *case history* approach, which derives from clinical practice.

The essence of this approach is that we gather sufficient information to present a detailed picture of an individual over a period of time. The time element, of course, enables us to look at causal factors in operation. This, too, is something which can exist on two levels, the natural and the manipulated. At its most natural, it is essentially an anecdotal method of providing insight. Again, it is something that we meet very often in general conversation and in discussion on the television, and so on. We may be interested in whether there is any truth in the saying 'Spare the rod and spoil the child'. The sort of informal observations we have already discussed ('I have been giving the cane to boys for thirty years and it hasn't done any of them any harm') can merge into an account of 'My sister Emily's boy – she never lifted a hand to them, you know, and by the time he was thirteen he'd been up before the

---

[1] It is also possible to deal with complex data by means of a number of statistical methods known as 'factor analytic techniques', but these are beyond the scope of an introductory book such as this is.

juvenile court three times!' The same method is to be found in a more considered and ordered form in biographies, or studies of the childhood of great men, and also in a sense in works of fiction which have a similar biographical form. It should be remembered, however, that novels about children do not have the same status as *evidence*. The view of the way personality develops may be the things that appears in the author's mind first, and the events of his character's life may then be cast to illustrate his view. It may be impossible to find a single place in real life where the same pattern is followed. Of course, the extent to which a novel is immune from this sort of criticism is one of the measures of its quality. But the point is worth making because literary examples are frequently drawn upon to 'prove' points connected with child development. The fact that such and such did not happen in David Copperfield's case is only admissible as a relevant consideration if we can demonstrate that there was an original for David Copperfield and that it happened to him.

The clinical case history is of course much more formal. Reports from a number of sources, the results of tests, and so on, are fitted together into as detailed as possible a picture of the subject's life. In this case, we can again assert that the situation has become artificial, or manipulated, since a number of people are intervening in order to collect and present the data.

The particular advantage of the case history is that not only does it permit us to draw conclusions about causal relationships, but that it can deal comfortably with aspects of development such as character and personality which are not always easy to assess by other, more objective, means. For this reason you will find that the method is to be found most frequently in works dealing with this branch of the subject and more particularly in books which concentrate on topics such as maladjustment and delinquency. This derives, too, from the connection between these latter topics and medical psychology, where the case history method had its main origins.

The weaknesses of this approach lie in its lack of control of the factors which may be causing the phenomenon under investigation. In this, it resembles the last group of methods discussed. It also has the disadvantage that the interpretation and the data may not be separated.

I have pointed out that this method of gathering data is particularly associated with studies of maladjustment and the like. There are, of course, obvious dangers in making a great use of atypical individuals as a source of information about the normal child. Case histories of neurotic children may show us that they all have some factor in common – some event or circumstance in early childhood. Their unanimity may lead us to suppose that this factor necessarily leads to neurosis, but this idea does not necessarily follow. We may find that the factor in question is found just as frequently in non-neurotic children. To take an absurd example, all neurotic children have been born, but we cannot say on that account that being born is a cause of being neurotic (though of course it does help).

Nevertheless, the case history method has considerable flexibility and sensitivity; these are its advantages. Perhaps its main disadvantage lies in the fact that a case history is only as good as the people who are compiling it.

We have seen that the question of establishing causal relationships is one which has caused us a certain amount of difficulty. To do this, we really need to control as many factors as possible, leaving, as the only variable, the factor under investigation. We then make a prediction in line with our hypothesis and see if it is borne out by the facts. To return to the question of vocabulary development. One way of providing data on the causal role of social class would be to select a group of children such that they were as alike as possible with regard to age, the proportions of the sexes in the groups, intelligence, type of school attended, and so on, leaving social class as the only difference between them. We could go further and match each individual in the high social class group with another in the low social class group, so that the make-up of the two groups was virtually identical for every other factor. We could then make our prediction, namely that if social class influences the development of vocabulary, there will be a significant difference between the scores of the two groups for our vocabulary test.

When we control factors in this way, we have passed beyond the method of making observations, and have begun instead to carry out *experiments*. This is the method which is best adapted to the investigation of causal relationships and it can provide the answer to a wide variety of questions from whether a particular method of teaching helps children to learn to read, to whether babies thrive better on breast or bottle feeding, or whether practice has anything to do with children learning to walk. Though it is not always expressed entirely clearly, such questions are all of the form 'Is A a cause of B?', or 'Is A associated with B?'

The experimental method is particularly favoured by those psychologists who like to think of their topic as a science. Unfortunately, it has a number of difficulties, which are of two kinds, practical and ethical.

In practice, the kinds of factor which play a part in questions to do with development are not always easy to control in the way I describe in the example given above. Real life situations contain an enormous number of variables. We can (if we are clever, or lucky) control for all the factors that we think of, but we cannot guarantee that we have thought of them all. Thus doubt was cast on a number of carefully carried out experiments about children learning to read because a new factor was discovered, namely the enthusiasm of the teacher. It was found that teachers who are enthusiastic about trying out a new method tend to produce better results, irrespective of the method.

Another point about the experimental approach is that, because of the conditions which need to be satisfied if control is to be established, it tends to be restricted to very specific questions, rather than to deal with broad issues. This sometimes leads the layman to regard the results as trivial and even pointless. Such a criticism, however, will often have less force if you take a broader view, placing the particular experiment in the wider context of other experiments carried out in the same area. Each finding may

then be seen to represent a small, specific advance, gaining significance from the numerous other findings. For example, we may
wish to answer the question, 'Why do some children develop
aggressive personality traits?' It would be impossible to devise an
experiment to answer this, but we could split the topic into
numerous specific questions, such as, 'Is frequent punishment
related to later aggressiveness?': 'Is there a connection between
family size and aggressive behaviour?': 'Do television programmes
bring about aggression?' Of course, a great many such inquiries
will be necessary before we have a comprehensive answer to the
original, general question, and the progress of experimentally
based research is necessarily extremely slow.

A further type of difficulty is concerned with ethics. In studying
child development we frequently come across questions of whether
something harms the growing child. This may be to do with
physical growth, as when we wish to find out whether certain
drugs may, if prescribed for the mother during pregnancy, produce disorders in the baby; whether deficiency of vitamin D produces rickets in growing children; or whether young children
deprived of affection or of maternal care tend to develop psycho-
pathic disorders, or become delinquent. There are no great difficulties of a technical kind in the way of finding out the answers
to such questions. We could dose one group of mothers with the
suspect drug while keeping another group free of it; we could
deprive one group of children of vitamin D or of maternal care
and look for significant differences between the way they developed and the development of another, non-deprived group
(provided, of course, that we controlled all the factors except the
one under investigation). The real difficulty is that no one would
contemplate in the first place carrying out experiments of this kind.

Such difficulties are not always insuperable. You will remember the two experiments on environmental stimulation described
in the introduction. The first one involved two children being
deprived of stimulation over a period of months, and we may ask
whether an experiment of this kind was justified. (The fact that
the experimenter reported no ill effects does not alter the argu-

ment; if it had been *known* beforehand that this would be the outcome, there would have been little point in doing the work.) The second experiment avoided this difficulty by using a different experiment design. Instead of exposing the children to massive and possibly damaging isolation, which would result in measurable deviations from the norm, the experimenters restricted themselves to looking for very small temporary changes, arising from limited periods of deprivation.

But not all questions are amenable to being dealt with in this fashion, and in these cases we may be able to have recourse to what are sometimes termed 'natural experiments'. That is, naturally occurring situations which reproduce as nearly as possible the conditions we would like to set up in a formal, or artificial environment. Thus, to investigate the effects of drugs given to the mother on the development of children, we might find a group of mothers who had been given the drug in the normal course of events, and compare the development of their children with those of mothers who had not taken the drug. Although this is ethically permissible, it does however lead to experimental difficulties arising from the fact that, as with all the 'natural' approaches to child study, we are no longer in control of the factors which may be helping to determine the result.

It is also useful to distinguish between *retrospective* and *follow-up* studies of child development. In the former, we start with the event whose development we wish to trace, and go back over its history in order to review the factors which may have given rise to it. Suppose that we wish to know why certain children do not learn to read. We may examine the histories of groups of readers and non-readers in order to find significant differences. This is, of course, a kind of natural experiment, and has the same difficulties as those we have already discussed, namely that an important factor may escape observation simply because we have no idea what to look for, or that a factor may appear to have a false significance due to our being wise after the event. Generally speaking, the follow-up study is a much more valid observation. In this case we make our observations at the beginning and continue them through the child's development. The main difficulty with work of this sort is essentially a practical one. If we are to carry it out on a reasonably large sample, in order to be sure of not being misled by studying an atypical individual, we may find that the research gets bogged down with a kind of detective work. Especially in a society like our own, people change jobs, move about from one part of the country to another, and sometimes even emigrate. It may be very difficult to follow up all the population in the original sample. This can lead to a distortion in the kind of evidence gathered. If we are not careful, our final sample will consist only of those people who tend to stay put, and these may differ in a number of important ways from the population as a whole.

To sum up, the first thing we need to do when looking at a book on child development is to decide which methods have been used to provide the data on which the picture of the developing child is based. I have tried to indicate that we should not regard some of them as right and others as wrong. Each of the methods has certain advantages and certain corresponding limitations. If the data presented in various books is in conflict, we can sometimes see the origin of the disagreement in the method used, and make appropriate allowances. For convenience, the material presented in this chapter is summarized in Table I.

	NATURAL	MANIPULATED
OBSERVATION	Informal observations by parents, teachers, etc.	Interviews. Tests. Mass observations. Structured observations.
CASE HISTORY	Anecdotal. Literary/historical.	Clinical.
EXPERIMENT	Natural Exp. (Retrospective or follow-up).	Formal Experiment.

Table I : Methods of child study.

two

The Idea of Development

In any subject it is important to begin by making sure that we understand just what the key words connected with that subject are going to signify. It can be argued that, provided we make it clear and are consistent about how we use them, we can make them mean anything we like. But there must be limits, of course, to this procedure, otherwise one ends up in the same position as Humpty Dumpty in *Through the Looking Glass*. When dealing with description of an actual process, which has an existence independent of any concepts we may apply to it, there are two factors which limit the scope of our definitions. On the one hand, we must pay attention to the usual meanings of a word, to the concepts which it normally carries; on the other, we must have regard to the nature of the phenomenon we are dealing with, since an inappropriate definition, if it is arrived at before we have enough of the facts at our disposal, may have an influence on what we report, and in extreme cases even on what we think we see.

To begin, then, we should form a clear idea of what we mean by 'development' in this context of the growing-up of children.

Perhaps we can illustrate the need for an adequate definition by looking at the effects of applying too constricted a meaning to the word. Until fairly recently, a common definition of development was one which started from the statement that 'to develop' means 'to unfold', and that the growth of the child was therefore essentially a process of unfolding of natural qualities and capacities. This definition was supposedly based on the derivation of the word (though in fact it is doubtful whether this derivation was philologically accurate; since development is more probably derived from the Latin for 'to remove a veil from'.) This seems to me to be an extraordinary basis for a statement on what is, after all, an empirical fact. The origins of a word are not necessarily an accurate guide to its modern usage. Still less are they a guide to the actual nature of the processes to which the word is applied. We are no more entitled to believe that the derivation of the word development indicates that we are dealing with an unfolding process than we are to believe that a silly mid-on is necessarily a pious cricketer, on the grounds that the word 'silly' derives from an Anglo-Saxon word, meaning saintly or holy – or, for that matter, that the process of development is essentially one of unveiling.

What are the consequences of adopting a definition of this kind? The idea of unfolding carries a number of implications. We have already, in adopting such a definition, built in the assumption that we are dealing with a process which is there to start with, something which is innately present. A prejudice of this sort may lead us to look particularly for changes of this kind, and to overlook events which do not fit into such a pattern, or even to force the data to fit in with our preconceptions. The trouble with a definition of this sort is that it is not only circumscribes our field of interest, but that it also has assumptions built into it dealing with the task of explanation. We should try to keep these things separate.

Suppose that we are concerned with the development of intelligence. The application of the definition given above could well lead us to presuppose that we are dealing with an *inherited* factor which 'unfolds' as the child grows older. For many years intelligence was usually thought to be an innate quality of this kind. In a later chapter, we will look at some of the evidence on this question: recent surveys and experiments have shown that the environment does play a very large part in determining the level of intelligence. The definition is inadequate because it makes it more difficult for us to grasp this, or restricts the field in such a way that the development of intelligence is by definition not development because it does not consist of an unfolding process.

And yet we cannot entirely overlook the usage of the word. A completely neutral definition, such as 'development means change over a period of time' is attractive in many ways, but it will not really do. When studying the development of any organism, we are surely not saying that we will be concerned with any change over time, no matter what its form. There seems something odd about saying that Whitby Abbey has, in the course of the last few hundred years, developed into a ruin; a busy railway system has developed into a single-branch line carrying one local train a day; or vultures have developed an animal's carcass into a skeleton. More typical are such examples as: a small business which develops into a large industry, a child who develops into a man, a politician who develops into a statesman, and so on. These examples might lead us to suppose that the key idea is one of improvement, but this is not necessarily the case: we can just as well talk about the development of a disease, the development of a threatening international situation, or of a serious balance of payments crisis. What is it that these ideas have in common? It seems to be the idea of an increase in extent, complexity or integration, or a combination of these.

The definition of development which these suggest is an attractive one. It clearly demarcates those changes we shall be studying from other kinds of change; we are looking for phenomena to do with the growth, organization and increase in the extent of the individual's attributes rather than at the inverse processes which characterize more typically pathology or old age (we might of course talk about the development of the symptoms of old age, but this is not an exception to the definition we have proposed, since, by changing the grammatical subject, we have brought it within the same usage). In addition to marking off our area of study, the proposed definition does not contain any assumptions about *how* the increases take place and so does not prejudice our empirical investigations.

We need, too, to be clear about what it is that is developing. Many child development books leave us in no doubt about this. We should be concerned, they tell us, with the development of the whole child. This is an easy instruction to give, but what exactly does it entail in practice? Let us see how it works out in a hypothetical case.

Jo Soap has recently entered the sixth form in his local secondary school. Physically, he is thin, pale and weakly looking. He is short-sighted and wears heavy framed glasses which give him the earnest look of an already middle-aged adolescent. A physical factor which does not show is that he has suffered since early childhood from a minor heart ailment. He is exceptionally good at maths, but probably a little below average at English and foreign languages. His social life is rather limited; he never goes to clubs or social functions and seems to be ill at ease except when with his few close friends. His lack of ease becomes acute embarrassment when he speaks to girls, which he almost never does since he attends a single-sex school. His emerging sex instincts manifest themselves only in dreams and private fantasies, which leave him with intense feelings of guilt.

Although his development has been going on for about sixteen years, there are still a number of practical questions which we can ask in addition to the obvious general question of how did he develop into the person he is today? Should he, we want to know, study maths at the university, as his teachers want him to? If he does, will he get a good degree? Should he become a teacher, as his father wishes? If he does, will he be able to overcome his lack of social facility enough to communicate with his pupils? Will he, as his mother wishes, find a nice girl and settle down?

Of course, we can only answer such questions by considering the answer to the more general question about his early life. It is not possible to isolate one period from the rest of the sequence and consider it meaningfully in isolation. This, then, can be one meaning of studying the whole person.

But we must also look at the relationship of his particular attributes and capacities. Let us start by considering his physical development. From an early age he suffered from his minor heart complaint. This was not serious, but his mother was always the worrying kind, and she would not let him play rough games with the other children. This has had an easily apparent effect on his physique, but its results go rather deeper. By the time he started school, he could no longer compete, even if he wanted to, in any of the games or tricks which confer prestige among children of that age. He tended to withdraw from that kind of competition and compensated for this by concentrating on achievements in fields where he could be on equal terms with other children – especially in maths, for most of the children in his class disliked the subject as much as he disliked games. They responded by calling him a swot, and this led him to withdraw even more from social contacts which would have led him to develop those skills which help us to get on with other people. We have not gone very far in our analysis of Jo Soap, but we have already demonstrated connections and interactions between physical, social and educational development.

But, although we can account for Jo Soap's application to school-work in terms of the combined effects of his physical handicap, and his mother's attitudes to it, on some aspects of his personality, this is not the whole story. We can not trace the development of his mathematical ability without reference to how his concepts of numbers and relationships have developed from the earliest, and most basic, ideas of quantity, to his present level of sophisticated mathematical reasoning.

Nor are the influences in one direction only. Given a sufficiently high level of achievement in his academic work – a First, say, at his university, followed by a job which has a good deal of prestige – scholastic success may give him confidence which can be transferred to his social life.

It seems, then, that child development is not in fact a single process of the kind we have defined, but much more like a matrix of simultaneous developments in a number of directions. To understand completely what is going on, we need to look at the total picture, since each of them affects all of the others. Looking back to the case of Jo Soap, it may be that even the small factor of his short-sightedness has played its part: recent research has shown a small, but significant connection between myopia and academic inclination.

But this is a counsel of perfection. In practice, the human mind is a limiting factor; we just cannot grasp so complex a picture. We must therefore usually content ourselves with examining a particular line of development in isolation – social, intellectual, emotional, and so on. The greatest concession we can usually make to the ideal course of studying the whole child is to keep an open mind and look for the intrusion of other aspects of development into the field we are examining.

There is, of course, no end to the degree of specialization which is possible. One book may deal with intellectual development as a whole, another may describe the development of the child's use of language, his understanding of number or the development of logical reasoning. Other researches may take this process even further and discuss the development of the understanding of words like *because* and *why*, or the concept of the conservation of matter. Similarly in other fields: there are general books on physical development and studies which look at the development of delicate muscular co-ordination or of athletic prowess, or the way in which the sexual impulses make their appearance.

We need to put in here a word of warning. Sometimes one meets writers on child development who talk about studying the 'whole child', when in fact they do not mean anything of the sort. Frequently when someone says, 'I am not concerned with physical or intellectual development, but with the development of the whole child', what is meant is, 'I am concerned with the development of the child's personality'. There is, of course, nothing wrong with being concerned with this aspect of development, but it is best to be clear at the outset about what is meant.

Is there any superiority in one way of looking at the problem as compared with another? Is the general approach superior to the specific one? There can be no absolute answer to such questions, since it depends entirely on what you are trying to do. If you are trying to write a maths course which will capitalize on the natural stages in the child's understanding of number, you can afford to take a very narrow view of child development; information about the development of the child's athletic ability is likely to be irrelevant. If, on the other hand, you are concerned with a subject like the sex education of younger teenagers, you would probably need to take a broader view which would include aspects of physical development, of emotional maturity, of social skills and probably information about the nature of their attitudes towards questions of right and wrong. You could, however, probably exclude information about their number concepts.

It has been said that, for the student of child development, people cease to exist as soon as they grow up. Like many such jibes, there is a good deal of truth in it, though it is fair to point out that to limit a field of study by calling it *child* development is necessarily to exclude development which takes place in adult life. Perhaps the proper moral to draw from this is that studies of the subject should not be limited in this way: we should think rather of *human* development, and seek to place our studies of children within this wider context.

This is all the more important when one bears in mind that even those writers who seem to take the narrower view of development frequently have in mind quite specific assumptions about what the end product is (or should be) like. Such assumptions should not be taken for granted; we should ask quite explicitly what the child is developing into.

Common sense tells us that this end product is the average, or normal, man or woman. Terms like 'maturity' or 'mental health' often tend to be thrown into discussion of the topic, giving it a scholarly, even authoritative air. The difficulty with such ideas is that it is so easy to use them in such a way that they mask quite large assumptions which may not be justified.

Physical development probably provides the clearest example. Our picture of the physically mature adult is determined by the people whom we see in our own society. This, we are tempted to say, is the norm. But it is easy to show that there are considerable differences in, say, height, between people belonging to different cultures, and even within the same culture at different times. In recent years the average height, strength and fitness of both men and women in most Western societies has increased significantly. This may of course be accounted for by better nutrition, proper exercise, and improving home conditions. But whatever caused it, developmental goals based on the norms of fifty years ago would be inappropriate today. In the same way, data about the physical development of children cannot easily be transferred between one society and another.

Similarly, there has been a trend in recent years whereby sexual maturity, at least in its physical aspects, is attained a couple of years earlier than was once the case. And differences in the age of onset of puberty are still to be found between one culture and another.

These examples have dealt with fairly obvious cases in which an assumption of similarity can be demonstrated to be untrue. Adults can be measured and shown to be so many inches taller than they used to be. Sexual maturity can be noted and its age compared with the ages that obtained thirty years ago. The dangers of generalizing from the norms of one's own culture are much greater in cases where there are no hard measurements to act as a corrective. When considering both personality development and the development of social roles, we are bound to be interested in the emergence of personality and social differences between the sexes. Little boys tend to develop traits like toughness, inquisitiveness, aggressiveness, independence, and so on. Little girls tend to be characterized by the qualities which we normally regard as being more feminine – they tend to be more tender-minded, dependent, and so on. These attitudes are so deeply embedded into the ideas we have about masculine and feminine attributes that we tend to regard them as being part of the very nature of sex itself. This leads us to suppose that they come about through the operation of innate factors rather than learning processes, and to expect them to be reflected in the development of children of whatever culture. But there are a few societies in which these 'natural' sex roles are reversed, places where the woman is the aggressive ruler of the family, the provider of food, the one who works in the fields while her passive and dependent husband stays at home and looks after the house. Clearly, any attempt to account for the way children develop in such a culture which was couched in terms of our own norms would be misleading. And, studying children in our own culture, application of fixed and stereotyped concepts of maturity could prevent us from noticing changes which may be taking place in such things as sex roles.

The point is not merely that one needs to take cultural norms into account when looking at development, but that one should be careful of how one uses apparently neutral words, like 'maturity' and 'mental health', since they are in fact all too often loaded with unexpressed values. It should not in principle be impossible to work out value-free usages for such words, but this is not the place to attempt such a task.

three

Patterns of Growth

WE HAVE defined development, in this context, as referring to increase in extent, complexity and integration of an individual's attributes. This, of course, does not provide information about *how* such an increase takes place. Are there, in fact, any principles governing development, any patterns in the process of growth?

Firstly, we must firmly set aside the obvious, but naïve, assumption that biological or psychological development takes place by a process of simple accumulation – growth in a straight line, as it were. That is, that development proceeds at a regular pace, the amount of development being proportional to the time elapsed.

But let us look at a few examples of what we should expect if this were the case: if a child is 5 ft 2 in. tall at the age of fourteen, and was 20 inches long (or tall) at birth, he has grown 42 inches in fourteen years, which – if development is regular – works out at three inches a year. Thus, he should be 23 inches at one year, whereas he is in fact likely to be about 28 inches or 29 inches. To look at this the other way round, if the growth rate of the first year of life were part of a pattern of regular annual increments, a fifteen-year-old would be about twelve feet tall.

Similarly, if a child has no words when he is born and 2,500 at the age of six, he would be likely to have about 1,250 words when he is three years old. In fact, a three-year old knows about 900 words.

The first principle which appears to govern biological growth is one of irregularity. We may consider this under two headings: irregularity of time and irregularity of proportion.

Irregularity of time

By this we mean that over a period of time growth does not continue at a uniform rate. Development tends to proceed in spurts which are separated by plateaux of much slower growth. Physical growth, for example, though it does not stop altogether until

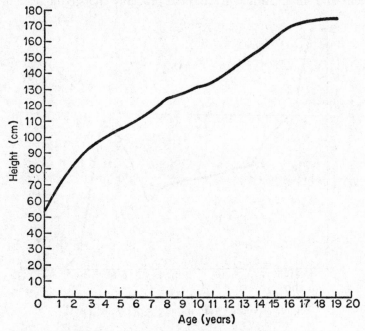

Fig. 1.   Average height of boys by age.

maturity, has two main periods during which it is much faster than in the intervening time. The first of these stretches through the pre-natal period and infancy into the toddler stage. The second occurs with adolescence.

If you look at a graph which shows the average height of children of different ages, such as is shown in Figure 1, your first reaction may be that it conforms fairly closely to the straight line progression which I have just argued is inappropriate. I have included this graph mainly to show how easy it is to come to mistaken conclusions from data which is not presented in the best way. In fact, any parent who gets Johnnie to stand with his back to the wall at regular intervals and puts a mark to show how much he has grown will tell you that the pattern is one of large gains and small. Although we could probably change the scale of

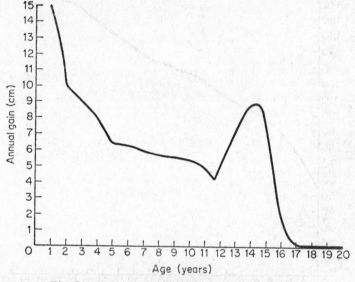

Fig. 2.   Average gain in height per year (boys).

the graph so that the irregularities show more clearly, it is probably easier – because we are talking about the *rate* of growth – to use a measure which shows this more directly. You can see a way of doing this in Figure 2. This again shows the average height of boys up to the age of twenty. As before, the figures along the bottom show the age in years, and those at the left-hand side show height. However, this time the height figure shows the average *gain* in height per year for each year of life. As you see, when the data is expressed in this form, the irregularities in time become very clear. You will notice how the rate of increase drops sharply until about three years old, when it levels off until the onset of adolescence, where there is a further rise. Figure 3 gives the average weight increase of girls in the same form. You will see that the same pattern of accelerated growth, slower growth followed by greater gains, is repeated in an even more exaggerated form.

A similar pattern can be seen in other forms of physical development. A particularly striking example of irregularity in

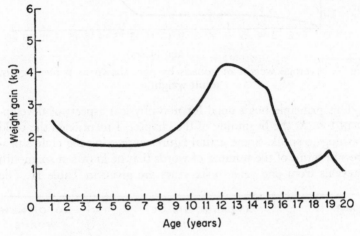

Fig. 3.   Average weight increase per year (girls).

normal development is given by the individual's sexual development. Although this is just as true of the development of sexual *behaviour* as it is of the physical aspects, the latter is easier to express numerically, so as to present a graph of the rate of growth. Figure 4 is a graph showing the individual's sexual development expressed in terms of the weight of the sexual glands at various ages. You will notice that the graph is almost horizontal from about two until the onset of adolescence, indicating that almost no growth at all takes place. Thereafter it rises sharply until maturity is reached.

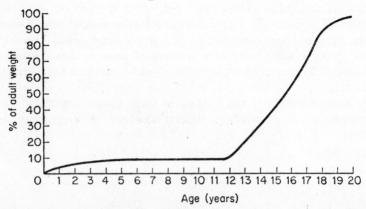

Fig. 4. Average weight of gonads by age, shown as percentage of adult weight.

This principle holds good for non-physical aspects of development too. At the beginning of the chapter, I mentioned the child learning to speak. Some actual figures expressing the child's progress in terms of the number of words that he knows at six month intervals from one year to six years are given in Table II. The

AGE	AVERAGE NO. OF WORDS	NO. OF NEW WORDS
1	3	–
1½	22	19
2	272	250
2½	446	174
3	896	450
3½	1,222	326
4	1,540	318
4½	1,870	330
5	2,072	202
5½	2,289	217
6	2,562	273

Table II: Growth of vocabulary from 1–6 years.

first column shows the age. The second column shows the size of his vocabulary. If you look at this column only, the irregularities are not immediately apparent. However, in the third column I have subtracted from each total the number of words the child

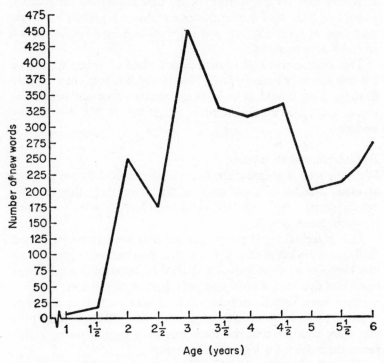

Fig. 5. Vocabulary growth: number of new words from 1 year to 6 years.

knew six months before, to show the number of new words he has acquired. It now becomes clear that the acquisition of vocabulary follows the same pattern of rapid growth interspersed with slower periods.

Figure 5 gives the same information, but in the form of a graph.

This irregularity of rate is apparent in many forms of learning, from riding a bicycle to learning typing or a foreign language. Progress, when it starts, is extremely rapid, but there soon comes a point after which no progress at all seems to be made for a time. It is very easy for the learner, or for that matter for the teacher, to become frustrated during this period, but it is probably a necessary time of consolidation, and it is followed by a further period of rapid improvement.

This characteristic of growth is described by many writers on the subject as 'discontinuity'. This word, however, can be misleading. You should bear in mind that it does not necessarily mean that growth discontinues altogether in the intervening periods.

Irregularities of Proportion
We have seen that many attributes of the individual are growing at once. Not all of these grow at the same rate; they are not synchronized – hence the technical term for this principle, which is 'asynchronous growth'.

This is something that you can actually see happening over a fairly short period of time if you watch the changes in proportions of a kitten or a puppy growing up. It does not start as a miniature version of the adult animal and get bigger in proportion. The proportions vary, sometimes from week to week, so that at one stage it seems to be all head, and at another time all legs. Sometimes you may even see that the back legs have been growing rather faster than the front legs, or vice versa.

To see the irregularities of proportion in the growth of a human being, we have to look at diagrams, such as that shown in Figure 6. Otherwise we would have to extend our observations over sixteen or seventeen years. Figure 6 shows the relative size of the head, as compared to the rest of the body, in children of different ages. You will see that, during the pre-natal period, the head must have been having a growth spurt; thereafter, its rate of growth slows down rapidly and the rest of the body catches up.

The word proportion does not refer simply to the proportions

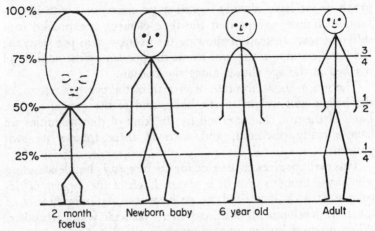

Fig. 6. Changes in the proportions of head, trunk and limbs, at four points in development.

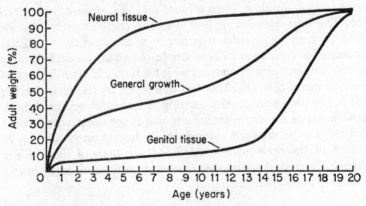

Fig. 7. Comparison of three growth rates.

of the body. It means that, proportionate to each other, different parts of the body, or even different functions, progress at different rates. This is illustrated in Figure 7. This is the same sort of graph as we have already looked at in connection with irregularities of time, except that the time element is expressed in a different way. Instead of showing the average gain per year, the left-hand column in this case shows the per cent of the adult level reached at the age shown along the bottom.

The graph shows the rate of growth of the nervous system, of the height and weight of the body, and of the genital organs. Each of them is characterized by the kind of discontinuities we have already discussed, and each of them follows its own pattern.

This perhaps gives us the clue for the best way of understanding what asynchronous growth is about. Each of the aspects of development is characterized, as we have seen, by irregularities or spurts in development, but these do not coincide with each other. When progress is slow, or stationary, in one direction, it is being made in another.

We have said that development is characterized by a movement from a simple state to a more complex, or more organized one. The next question is, how does this come about? Does the child proceed by putting together separate units, or by differentiating between holes? For example, the adult can perform very precise and complex operations with his limbs. He can fly an aircraft or mend a watch. Has this developed by the child having learnt precision and control starting from undifferentiated mass movements of his entire body? Or was it the other way round? Did he start with small movements of fingers and build up to control of the body as a whole? In fact, both of these things happen. We can describe them as two principles of development which are interdependent.

Differentiation

As we have seen, growth is in the direction of the simple to the complex. We start with single undifferentiated functions which then branch out and specialize. The process is, of course, to be seen in its most dramatic form in the growth of the human body, which starts as a single undifferentiated cell and grows into a complex human being with many different kinds of tissue: brain, skin, bone, etc., which serve different functions. In the very earliest stages of its development, before differentiation has gone very far, the cells of the embryo are identical with each other and are interchangeable. If a cell which would ultimately grow, by division, into an arm, could be moved to some other part of the new organism, it would develop into say, an eye or a leg, according to what was appropriate. Differentiation of function soon, however, eliminates this interchangeability.

Similarly, in the development of physical co-ordination, the child starts off by making mass movements; differentiation comes about gradually, coarse movements of large muscles preceding the appearance of fine movements by small muscles. Watch a child learning to write: the pre-school child is capable only of making large patterns on the paper which involve movement of the whole arm or forearm. From there, he moves to a stage when smaller movements come about, controlled through the wrist. Only at a very late stage do the fine finger controlled writing or drawing movements appear.

Integration

At the same time those things that have been differentiated – whether they are structures in the body or items of behaviour – tend to become integrated into new larger units which have characteristics of their own.

We can see this in physical development: the cells of the embryo gradually evolve into the differentiated structures of the liver, the stomach, the intestines and other organs which have to do with eating and digestion. But they have only a very limited function before birth: the child's main source of nourishment in the womb is of course not dependent on eating and digestion. After birth, the baby begins to take in food through his mouth, and these separate units become integrated into a digestive system.

We can see how both principles have a part to play. Structures or organs are formed by a process of differentiation. They are then fitted together into new larger structures.

This pattern is to be seen on the level of behaviour as well as in the development of physical organs. Reading gives a clear example of this. The child starts by recognizing writing as writing, but he cannot attach any meaning to individual symbols. He then associates particular stories with particular books and may go through the motions of reading a story, turning the pages at the proper time, but not doing anything which could properly be described as being reading. Reading proper emerges when the child begins to know a few words. At first, he responds only to whole words, working on their general appearance; they are, in other words, not yet differentiated. Reading becomes fully differentiated when the child is able to recognize the component units out of which words are built. We then move into a stage of synthesis. Knowledge of phonic units enables the child to build new reading patterns, so that he can read words which he has not seen before. Whereas reading is at first an achievement, an end in itself, it eventually becomes subordinated to other activities: it becomes part of general study patterns, or recreational patterns, and so on.

Developmental Directions

The direction of growth can be described in terms of two principles:
(i) It tends to proceed from the head towards the feet. This is described as *cephalocaudal direction*. (ii) Growth tends to proceed from the centre of the body towards the extremities. This is referred to as *proximodistal direction*.

Again, we can see these most clearly in the physical development of the embryo. The head forms long before the limbs make their first appearance; the arms begin to develop before the legs. The limbs themselves develop according to the second principle. They appear first as an arm or a leg bud and grow out towards the extremities; the fingers are among the last things to be differentiated. In behaviour, too, we see that the child is able to raise his head before he can control the trunk muscles involved in sitting up, and he can sit up before he develops enough control of the leg muscles to stand or walk.

These principles of development characterize development as a whole and not merely the development of the human being. They characterize the course of evolution just as much as the growth of the human child. This has led people in the past to suppose that, in the pre-natal period, the child has to recapitulate the entire history of the species, starting as an amoeba, and becoming a fish, and so on. It is perhaps truer to regard the striking similarities between different stages in the development of the human foetus and these various forms of life as being due to the operation of the same laws rather than to the fact that the human being has ever literally been one of these things.

To sum up:
    We have then seen four principles which seem to describe the universal tendency of development.
(i) Development is irregular in its rate (discontinuity of growth rate).
(ii) The different aspects of development do not keep pace with each other (asynchronous growth).
(iii) Development proceeds by specialization of simple structures and processes (differentiation).
(iv) These differentiated structures are reorganized into new larger units (hierarchic integration, hierarchization or functional subordination).
    Development tends to be in two directions.
(i) Growth tends to be in the direction of head to foot (cephalocaudal), and
(ii) from the centre of the body to the extremities (proximodistal).
(These last are frequently referred to as growth gradients.)

four

Born or Made?

WHEN DOES the individual's development start? At birth? At conception? Before?

It would clearly be nonsense to talk about the individual, as such, developing before he even exists, and yet a large part of the influences which shape his development do in fact date from before his conception. I am referring, of course, to the individual's genetic make-up. This is an important topic, which has a bearing on every aspect of the child's development. Why is one child a budding athlete and another a weakling – is it a question of constitution, or training? Why does one develop into a brilliant scholar, and another into a dullard? Are criminals born or made? We can only begin to answer such questions by considering the facts of heredity.

Unfortunately, we find that there is a great deal of ignorance and misunderstanding about the subject.

A major part of the difficulty arises from the kind of language which has come to be used about it in everyday speech, language which embodies concepts and models which are far removed from the actual laws of genetics. The use of words like 'inheriting' parents' characteristics predisposes us to visualize the process as something akin to the inheritance of money or property, an analogy which has led people to make such mistakes as to think that a parent can 'pass on' to a child (notice how the inappropriate image creeps in again) characteristics which the parent has acquired in his own lifetime. Again, the medieval notion of the blood as the carrier of genetic material lingers in our everyday speech – 'He hasn't a drop of Negro blood in his veins' – which leads some people to make all kinds of erroneous suppositions about the effects of mixed marriages.

The first point to make is perhaps that heredity appears to operate in a different fashion from most other aspects of development. In nearly every book on children, you will find that it is stressed, and quite rightly, that people are not to be fitted into pigeon holes. You cannot fit people into categories of good people and bad, clever people and stupid, any more than you can put them into categories of tall people and short. There exist not only the well-defined extreme cases, but also a continuum of fine discriminations stretching between them, and to assess a person's goodness or intelligence or height, we must place them on this continuum.

This concept of the continuous dimension is something which we meet so often in our studies of human beings that we may be tempted to apply it to everything affecting them, but it does not apply in the case of heredity. Heredity is discrete, or particulate. Of course, faulty models of the hereditary process, such as the idea of 'blood', make it easier for us to misunderstand this. Blood, we may imagine, can be diluted with 'other bloods' to an infinite degree, so that we can think of someone being one eighth Negro or one sixteenth Irishman, and so on.

However, the process does not work in this way. Hereditary characteristics are controlled by *genes*, a name which was made up to indicate the carriers of genetic material long before people had any idea of what the actual mechanism was by which genetic transmission took place. Genes work rather like a binary system in a computer; the gene governing a particular characteristic is either present or absent, and there are no other possibilities. At first sight, this may seem to be an oversimplification, ruling out the possibilities of hybrids, but a brief consideration of the laws of genetics will show that this is not so. It will be easier, however, to see how this works out if we first take a look at the actual mechanism by which hereditary transmission takes place.

The cells of which the human being is composed are forty-six *chromosomes*, arranged in twenty-three pairs. These chromosomes carry the genes. We now know that transmission is governed by a complex substance, known as D N A, which is in each of the chromosomes. D N A is a complex molecule formed from four main organic substances. The arrangement of these substances is in effect a code or template, containing instructions about how the individual should develop. It is easier, of course, for us to visualize how this works than it was to find it out in the first place. The D N A molecule is described as a double helix, that is, it is in the shape of two corkscrews intertwined. The four substances making the code are arranged along these spiral threads, and they give information somewhat after the fashion of the morse code. The morse code has only two symbols, a dash and a dot, and yet when these are arranged in sequences, they are capable of transmitting every word in every language that uses our type of alphabet. The genetic code works with four symbols and twenty-three pairs of chromosomes, each containing hundreds of thousands of genes. Clearly, the amount of information it can carry must be unimaginably large.

Mathematicians have sometimes worked out the number of possible genetic combinations. The formulae for finding the number of possible permutations or combinations of a given number are very simple – thousands of people use them every week in their football coupons – so it is simple in principle to find a number which represents the number of genetic types theoretically possible. The trouble with such numbers is that, like the distances in the universe between various galaxies, they are so large that it is difficult to attach any real meaning to them. Let us simply say, then, that the number of genetic possibilities can be shown to exceed at the most conservative estimate the probable number of every human being who has ever existed or is now alive; and possibly it is greater than the number of atoms in the solar system. This is the kind of backing for statements about the uniqueness of every individual. The chances against two individuals (apart from identical twins) being alike are so great that it is not possible to comprehend them. And remember that we are only talking about *genetic* differences – we have said nothing about the effects of the individual's experience as he goes through life.

The code, then, for these genetic differences is carried in the DNA molecule. It is thought that the two spiral arms separate, rather as if you were to twist a ladder into a spiral, and then saw through each rung. Each half can then complete itself.

The detailed relationship between genes and physical and intellectual characteristics is, for the most part, not yet known in

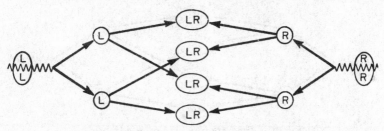

Fig. 8. The honeysuckle and the bindweed.

detail. It is known that one chromosome determines the sex of the new child. Another is known to be associated with Mongolism; a third, as we shall see below, is suspected of causing some kinds of criminality.

To return to the human cell's forty-six chromosomes, twenty-three are provided by each parent. The specialized cells which are destined to form another individual – the spermatozoa and the ova – have, however, only half of this number, so that when they combine, they form a new genetic pattern which will be a new individual with the normal set of forty-six chromosomes. To form these specialized reproduction cells, then, the chromosomes must split into two halves. Now, the important point is that they revert to the original patterns of genes provided by the individual's own parents.

An example will make this clear. You may know the song about the left-handed honeysuckle and the right-handed bindweed. Figure 8 shows how it would work out if such a mating

were actually to take place. Let us suppose that the direction of
the plant's growth is determined by a single gene. Presuming that
both the honeysuckle and the bindweed were themselves genetically pure, the genes provided by each set of parents are the same
(shown in the diagram as L L for the left-handed gene and R R
for the right-handed gene). When these are split to form the
gametes (the reproductive cells) the only split possible is, as shown

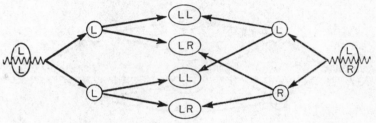

Fig. 9.   The honeysuckle and the hybrid.

in the diagram, two left-handed genes for the honeysuckle, and
two right for the bindweed. The only possible combinations involve one gene of each kind, so all the offspring are genetically
mixed (L R) and 'grow straight up and fall flat on their face'.

But what will happen in the next generation? Let us suppose
that an L R plant is crossed with another left-handed honeysuckle.
This is shown in Figure 9. The honeysuckle forms gametes as
before, but the hybrid plant must split its chromosomes to form
an L and an R. This gives us two possible combinations. Another
hybrid, like the parent, or a fully left-handed plant, which has no
right-handed genetic content at all. The right-handedness has
disappeared as though it had never occurred in the pedigree.

Thus, each new individual is compounded of new variations of
his parents' genetic material. To understand how this takes place
is to see at once why the *acquired* characteristics of the parents
cannot be passed on to their children. A parent cannot, by taking
a body-building course, cause his children to inherit strong

muscles, or by learning French, cause his child to inherit linguistic ability. Put like this, the proposition perhaps sounds absurd, but it is one which has been given widespread support even in very recent times. In the Stalinist era, a number of Russian scientists were dismissed from their posts for arguing that this form of inheritance was impossible.

Heredity and Environment

We turn now to the question of the part played by heredity in the growing child. For some reason, many people find it necessary to draw up lines of battle on this question, to regard themselves as environmentalists or hereditarians. The debate has gone on for close on a century now, and it still re-echoes, even though there is a great deal of evidence for anyone who cares to look for it. And questions of this sort are more frequently settled by evidence than by debate.

In a radio discussion on the treatment of delinquency, I heard a lawyer (slipping, perhaps, into his courtroom manner) hectoring a criminologist: 'Come now, you must believe that delinquency is either inherited or learnt. It must be one or the other. Which do you think it is?'

Even to put the question in this form is to force the issue into a simplicity which is almost grotesque.

The fact is, of course, that the individual's characteristics are determined by both heredity and environment acting together. Figure 10 shows how this interaction takes place. Note the considerable overlap between the two genetic types shown.

Geneticists have found it useful to distinguish between the *genotype* and the *phenotype*. The genotype is the individual's genetic constitution, derived from his parents and passed on to his children. The phenotype is the individual's characteristics as we observe them, the individual as he is developed by the influence of the environment on the genotypic material, which you may regard perhaps as the individual's inherent potential. A man who has genotypic strength will not develop into a weightlifter without proper food and exercise, and at the level of the phenotype, he may be surpassed by someone who is genetically less inclined to be muscular, but who has adequate amounts of both.

The interaction between hereditary and environmental factors

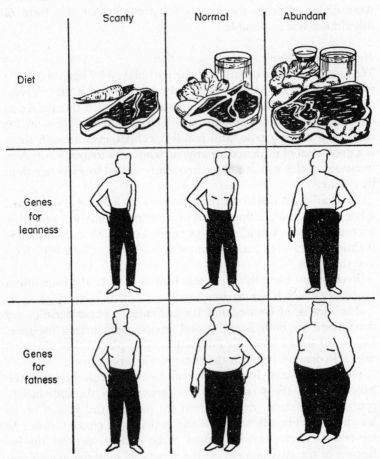

Fig. 10. Gene-environment interaction. A person who has a gene for 'fatness' may actually weigh less than a person with a gene for 'leanness', if the former lives on a scanty and the latter on an over-abundant diet.

begins almost as soon as the baby is conceived. The statement is sometimes made that pre-natal influences are all hereditary, but a moment's thought will show that this cannot be the case. Although there is no truth in the sort of old wives' tale which said that if the mother was frightened by a mouse, the baby would have a mouse-shaped birthmark, pre-natal environmental effects have been demonstrated only too clearly. German measles contracted by the mother at a certain point in pregnancy can cause cataract, deafness, or death in the developing foetus. We know, too, of the effects on unborn babies of the drug thalidomide.

We must note here the difference between *congenital* conditions and those that are *inherited*. Thalidomide babies suffer from congenital handicaps – that is, they are born with them. But the handicap is due to the harmful action of a drug, and not to any hereditary factors. Similarly, though Mongolism[1] is known to be associated with a chromosome irregularity, it has been shown that it is related to the age and physical condition of the mother, rather than to her genetic characteristics.

Interaction, then, begins before birth and continues through the person's life. Genetics determine the limits of the child's development; the environment determines the degree to which they are approached.

How much does each of these factors contribute? To answer this, experiments have been carried out on the intelligence of twins. As many readers already know, twins are of two kinds, identical and fraternal. Identical twins come about when one fertilized cell splits to form two individuals. The genetic constitution of these two individuals is identical, because of the way they were formed. Fraternal twins, on the other hand, are formed by two spermatozoa fertilizing two ova at the same time, and the twins are not any more similar genetically than brothers and sisters formed through fertilization on widely separate occasions.

[1] Mongolism is a developmental disorder characterized by stunted growth and extreme mental defect – and usually also by a very affectionate disposition.

We have, then in the comparison of identical and fraternal twins, a good example of the natural experiment.

Surveys of various kinds have been devised to take advantage of this situation. Many of them have been concerned with the roles of heredity and environment in the determination of intelligence. Comparisons of the relationship between the intelligence of twins have shown that identical twins are more nearly alike in intelligence than are fraternal twins. It can be argued that, though the environment is never really alike for any two people, the environment of twins is as similar as you are likely to find, and the result shows that heredity is an important factor.

On the other hand, investigators have found identical twins who, due to some circumstance like the death of their parents, have been brought up in widely separated environments. In these cases, the difference between their intelligence levels is much greater – in extreme cases the difference may be as great as 20 or 30 I Q points. These studies demonstrate clearly that environment, too, plays a part. On the basis of the examination of a large number of cases like those described in the preceding two paragraphs, most authorities have decided that about two thirds of the variation in intelligence is due to heredity, and one third to environment. This may seem to be saying that hereditary factors are preponderant, but it is still true that differences in the remaining third can make substantial differences to a child's educational prospects and his future career.

Not that this two-thirds ratio has any magic properties. It has been found in the case of intelligence. Something similar clearly operates in the case of height: Japanese children born and brought up in the United States are, though genetically similar, significantly taller than those brought up in Japan; but, for other characteristics, the genetic component may be stronger or weaker. Mongolism, though not inherited, is due to a disorder of the genetic material; its occurrence is not susceptible to post natal environmental influences.

An interesting new development has been the discovery of an apparent link between chromosome irregularities and criminality.

An irregularity in the sex determining chromosomes in men has been found to be very much more frequent among criminals with records of aggressive behaviour than among the normal population, and there is other evidence to show that there may be a causal link. But here again the abnormality has, in a very few cases, been found among non-criminals, so we are dealing with another case of interaction between heredity and environment, except that, in this case, the role of environment seems to be less prominent.

It is depressing to notice that even here, where the evidence is recent and clearly set out, it is (wilfully?) misunderstood by those who need to set up the old debate again. Geneticists, they say, claim that criminals are born, not made; and they go on to pour scorn on the idea, or to say, 'I told you so.' In fact, geneticists, as you have seen, say nothing of the sort. A certain kind of criminality appears to be predominantly, but not exclusively, due to a genetic factor; other cases, they would readily admit, exist where the emphasis is reversed. Life is not organized like a debating society.

five

The Normal Child

AT THE beginning of this book we looked at a number of short examples of different approaches to developmental study. One of these concerned the six-year-old child. His emotions, we were told, swing from one extreme to the other; he is beginning to recognize written words, and so on. This is an example of the kind of study which uses *norms*. These are so common that it is important to be sure of exactly what they are meant to be.

Norms make their appearance in all kinds of contexts. We have tables showing the proper weight of babies from month to month, norms for their increases in height, and a large class of statistically based figures, known as quotients, such as intelligence quotients, developmental quotients, which are a slightly disguised version of the same thing. Figures of this sort can cause considerable worry to parents, who may read, for instance, that at the age of one and a half years the child knows twenty-two words. Try as they might, they can't make Johnnie's vocabulary greater than twenty (and this is probably including a number of indeterminate sounds). Does this mean that he is abnormal? Mentally deficient, perhaps? Similar agonizing takes place over weight and over the lists of ages which are the norms for acquiring various skills.

But what exactly is a norm? Clearly, it does not mean that every six year old is learning to read, or is subject to wide swings of behaviour. It does not mean that *every* year-and-a-half-old infant knows twenty-two words. Unfortunately, those who use the term are not always as precise as they should be about what they do mean. This is important because the word can be used in various ways.

Perhaps the most important distinction to be made is that between the norm as a statistic, based upon actual averages of a particular population, and the norm as a criterion, based upon considerations of function, as in discussing physical or mental health. The two, of course, are not by any means the same thing. We see this very clearly in some of the underdeveloped countries, where malnutrition is statistically the norm. The weights of children as they develop, their level of activity, their speed of learning, all may be retarded by comparison with their Western counterparts. In some areas, the statistical norm may be so far depressed that the child is barely maintained at a level where normal living is possible. But this does not mean that such malfunctioning should be regarded as normal in the physiological sense. In the Middle Ages in Europe, it was sometimes known for vitamin deficiency diseases, such as scurvy, to become almost universal at the end of a hard winter. This statistical norm, then, would reflect the fact that a very large part of the population was ill. But again, using the word in a prescriptive sense we cannot regard such a state of affairs as being normal.

This, then, is the first point to decide in discussions about the normal child. Are we talking about statistical norms, or prescriptive ones? The distinction is often blurred because in an advanced society where there exist the material facilities for caring for children and ensuring optimal development, the dramatic distinction between statistical and prescriptive, which we have seen in less developed cultures, may not exist. But it does not follow from this that the distinction can be overlooked.

The normal weights for babies give an interesting example of this. Tables of norms are usually worked out in the first place by taking the average weight for babies of each age throughout the country concerned. In countries where there is a highly organized welfare service, most babies are weighed and measured at frequent intervals, and the average can be determined quite accurately. But in recent years, as our society has become more prosperous, people have tended to spend more on luxury foods, and children have come in for their share of these. The result is that more and more children in our kind of society are overweight, with, we are told, considerable resulting risks to health. Now, if we go on calculating the norms purely on a statistical basis, the average must go up, so that it becomes statistically normal to be overweight. A further misunderstanding allows such a statistic to be interpreted as a goal.

I knew a physical education teacher who, trying to come to grips with a similar problem to this, remarked that '90 per cent of the children nowadays are below average'. Mathematically, of course, this is nonsense. But one sees the problem that he is trying to get at. His error was in invoking a statistical, instead of a prescriptive, norm. The point is that in cases of this sort we must be sure which one we are dealing with.

It also follows that statistical norms are fluid, and that they vary not only from time to time, but from one country to another. The normal height for Scandinavian children is quite different from that for, say, Japanese children of the same age. This should be obvious, but the danger may be concealed. It is a trap we are particularly likely to fall into in the English-speaking countries where books may obtain a very wide circulation in areas which have the same language, but marked differences in culture, physique, or social custom. Very many American textbooks are in use in Britain and the Commonwealth countries. There is no reason why this should not be so, but care should be taken in applying norms. This is particularly true if we are considering something like social development. The social conditions in Britain may be quite different from those in America, and any attempt to transfer the normal social behaviour at a given age from one country to another could be most misleading.

A further problem exists where there are markedly separate groups within a main population. These groups may be racial in origin, as with the Negro community in the United States, and the various immigrant communities in Britain. It might be highly misleading to draw conclusions about members of minority groups which are based upon the averages for the population as a whole. Thus, a child who has spent a number of formative years in a country which is technologically unsophisticated may lag behind the average English child in the development of his understanding of mechanical cause and effect. This statistic, however, means just that, and not that the immigrant child is in some way retarded in his general intellectual development.

We have talked a great deal about the statistical norm and have seen some of its limitations, but there remain a number of questions. In particular, just what is the nature of the statistical norm? Clearly, a child who deviates by two or three words from the average vocabulary for his age is not going to cause us much concern, but what exactly are we saying when we make a statement of this kind?

Statistical norms are usually averages. We have seen some of the limitations which arise from the use of averages, and which reflect the fact that you can only usefully work out averages for particular populations. But there is a positive side, too. Naturally occurring phenomena of the sort that we are discussing here always follow a particular pattern. Look at the graph in Figure 11. It represents the average intelligence of a population of schoolchildren. The line along the bottom is marked off in intelligence quotients, and the vertical one at the left shows the percentage of the population which attains a given intelligence. Notice the symmetrical bell-shape of the curve. The average is in the middle at the highest point and the curve descends symmetrically at each side.

For a detailed discussion of distributions of this kind, you should look at a book on statistics. All we shall do here is to assert that this kind of distribution enables us to make certain predictions about how many of the population fall within a certain distance of the average. In other words, what we are saying is that if the average vocabulary of an eighteen-month-old baby is twenty-two words, exactly half of the babies in the country know more than this, and exactly half of them know less. Further, we know that the majority of them are clustered around this average, falling in predictable proportions measured out from the average.

Averages of this sort are sometimes used to make quotients. To do this, you need to have a list of average attainments for children of different ages. If a given child can solve problems which the average child of eight can do, we say he has a mental age of eight. If we divide this mental age by his actual (chronological) age, we have a quotient which expresses the child's achievement in comparison with that of the average child. Because fractions can be awkward to deal with, we nearly always multiply this quotient by 100, so that the answer is a kind of percentage. To return to the child with a mental age of eight, if his chronological age is also eight, then he has a quotient of 100. If, on the other hand, he is only six years old, the quotient would be 133, and if he were ten, the quotient would only be 80. The average is, of course, always 100, at least in theory, since that is what the quotient means. In practice, of course, there are likely to be slight variations resulting from the kinds of difficulties we have already discussed – changes over a period of time, or between one population and another.[1]

The usual quotient we see is the I Q or intelligence quotient. This is quite simply a comparison of the child's intellectual achievement with the average. Since there is a tendency for I Q to be constant – that is, those children who start out above the average tend to go on above the average – it is a very useful figure, particularly in trying to make decisions about a child's future. But there is nothing magic about it. It remains a statistical norm subject to the kinds of limitations we have already discussed and whenever we are using, or even talking about, the I Q, this should always be borne in mind. Quotients of this kind can be worked out for a wide variety of the child's activities. The one which is most relevant to our present subject is the developmental quotient which was mentioned in one of the experiments referred to at the beginning of the book. This is precisely the same kind of figure as the I Q, except that it is based not upon intellectual problem solving but on a wide variety of small achievements, such

[1] In practice, this method is not so often used nowadays in the construction of tests, which are based directly on the mathematical properties of the normal distribution shown in Fig. 11.

as whether a baby has reached the stage of being able to recognize
individuals, whether he can pick up objects with a finger and
thumb, whether he can aim food accurately into his mouth,
whether he can walk without assistance, and so on.

We have seen that such figures are based upon the use of

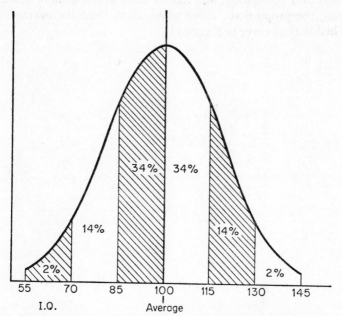

Fig. 11. The normal distribution curve: distribution of
intelligence.

statistical norms. They are, of course, giving the same information
as the age tables mentioned at the beginning of this chapter, but
expressing it in a different way. Naturally, the age tables themselves are subject to the normal distribution curve. If we say that
a baby of eighteen months has twenty-two words in his vocabulary, we are talking about an average, and a normal distribution
curve, which can be looked at in two ways. If we take all of the
one-and-a-half-year-old children, we find that twenty-two words

is the average; half of them know more words, half of them know less, the proportions falling away in the same pattern as that for height in Figure 11. Alternatively, we can say that the most frequent age at which people know twenty-two words is eighteen months, and that half of the children take longer than this to achieve this vocabulary, and half of them attain it more quickly. Again, the proportions, as we move away from the average, fit the bell-shaped curve in Figure 11.

six

Phases of Development

A CONVENIENT way of organizing data about development is to regard the child as going through a number of stages or phases. We shall be looking later in some detail at two approaches to child development which make use of a model of this kind.

Let us construct a phase sequence, using as our example the child's learning to speak.

In the first phase, he goes in for imitative babbling. He makes sounds like ma-ma-ma and pa-pa-pa. At this stage, no meaning at all is attached to the sounds, in spite of the delighted response of his mother, who tells all her friends that he said Ma-ma. (In fact, the formation of the word may well be the other way around. It may be that the babyish word for mother is, in so many languages, something like ma-ma simply because this is one of the first sounds that a baby naturally utters.)

However, to say that the baby's 'talking' at this stage is without meaning is not to say that this behaviour has no part to play in the development of language. The baby is learning to make the basic sounds of which his language is composed. We call these basic units 'phonemes', and of course they are different for different languages. We may regard this phase as being one of experimentation, at least as far as the formation of sounds is concerned. It is at this stage that the foundations are laid for the child's future ability to sort out and make the characteristic sounds of his own language. This, of course, is a fundamental, and to an adult often a difficult procedure. The Englishman very often has great difficulty in pronouncing French nasal vowels; the Italian may find it almost impossible to make the palatalized consonants used in Russian. To the speaker of a Semitic language, like Arabic, the final sounds in 'lick' and 'lock' are entirely separate consonants, a distinction which is simply not heard by most Europeans. The basis for this sort of ability is laid in this early phase of imitative babbling.

Phase two begins when meaning starts to be added. There comes a point when ma-ma is associated in some way with the idea of mother. We cannot exactly say that the child is using words, or that he is communicating. We are still at a stage of experimentation, but instead of the basic sound units, or phonemes, we are now dealing with morphemes, that is the basic meaningful units of language. I said that the child is not yet communicating. Although ma-ma is a response to the sight of his mother, and is correctly applied, the child does not yet use the word either to attract his mother's attention or to call for her when she is not there.

Phase three begins when the morphemes start to be used as ordinary words. By this, I mean that the child begins to make use of them as a medium for communication. As yet, his communications are limited to one word at a time, and they cannot be regarded as sentences in the grammatical sense. He may call 'din' or 'nunsh' when he wants feeding, 'bye-bye' when he wants a visitor to go home, and so on.

Phase four comes with the emergence of recognizable sentences, which begin to conform to the normal structure of the language. Thus, in English and other European languages you begin to see subjects and verbs, and so on. This, of course, is a break-through, and language growth accelerates at a fantastic rate at this point.

It is of course possible to enumerate many more stages after this – the discovery of further parts of speech, the use of subordinate clauses to imply causal, adverbial and other connections, the use of figurative or symbolic language, and so on. Or we can distinguish phases whereby the child uses language to obtain satisfaction of his needs, or to communicate ideas to other people. But the four phases of early language development, described above, are sufficient to illustrate our present argument. We can call them the stage of phonemes, the stage of morphemes, the stage of simple communications, and the stage of sentences.

Now there are two points to be made about such a model. The first is looking back at what we had to say in an earlier chapter. I referred to studies of language development which are based upon counting the number of words that a child knows. The present kind of analysis is more concerned with the *kind* of words that the child knows. Again, I would like to make the point that you cannot say that one approach is better than the other. Of course, it would be possible to combine them, and say that in phase three, which happens on the average at, say, two and a quarter years, the child knows 280 words, of which so many are nouns, so many are verbs, and so on. But this is needlessly complex for most purposes. It may be done for purposes of detailed study, but a great deal of insight can be gained by applying a simple model, such as the one described above.

The next point is to do with the idea of phases itself. Although there would, in principle, be nothing to stop you regarding a list of phases as simply representing what a child does within certain periods which are fairly clearly demarcated from one another, in practice we are usually saying rather more than this. We usually regard a sequence of phases as being a ladder or hierarchy. The child always goes through them in the same order, and, in a proper phase sequence, this holds good in spite of any individual variations of timing, such as we discussed in connection with the use of norms. Usually, when we are talking about phase sequence, we mean that it is impossible for the developing child to go through them in any order but the one described. It is as if you were describing someone going through the front door of a four-storey house with the intention of going up the stairs to the attic. He must be on the ground floor, first floor, and second floor, in that order. There is no other choice open to him. Of course, he can change his mind and go back downstairs again to a lower floor. Children do this too in their development. We call this process regression. The point is that it, too, fits in with the model we are using.

In stressing the idea that the child must go through the phases in a certain inevitable sequence, we are putting them in a relationship to each other which is usually a causal one. That is, they are not merely consecutive, but the successful attainment, or working through of each phase is necessary for the attainment of the next. In language development, the child has to be able to make phonemes in order to be able to attach meanings to them; he has to be able to use and understand words in order to string them together and pass into the phase of making sentences.

This, you might say, is a matter of common sense and everyday observation. But common sense and everyday observation can, on occasion, be very misleading. The idea of a sequence of phases as a causal ladder is one which fits very many developmental situations, but we must not be rash in applying it everywhere.

Let us look at the development of another babyish activity, namely learning to walk. If you observe a child over a period of eighteen months, you may make a number of observations which fit in very well with the sort of pattern described for language. The infant starts off by making random movements with his limbs; these, you may say, serve the sort of experimental function which we ascribe to babbling. He then begins to raise his trunk from the prone position and learns to sit unsupported. He moves on to two stages of locomotion, first wriggling almost prone along the ground with a kind of swimming motion, and then crawling on hands and knees. Finally, he is able to stand erect, and to walk with, and then without, support. These are reported in approximately the right order. Perhaps before reading further, you might like to try arranging them for yourself in a plausible sequence of phases.

Now there are two difficulties here, and each of them, even taken alone, can cause great problems when you are describing a child's development. Firstly, the simple act of naming the end product – being able to walk – is likely to govern our thinking, so that we talk about a single developmental sequence. I imagine that many readers will have constructed a model along these lines. But it does not follow that such a model is the best fit for the facts. What if we are dealing with not one, but two end products? If this is so, we ought surely to be thinking of two sequences, which go on at the same time. In the case of the child learning to walk, may there not be one sequence to do with acquiring an upright stance, and another to do with the idea of locomotion, both of them being combined in the final phase? Note that I am not raising the red herring of whether it is 'true' or not that there are really two sequences instead of one; I am simply suggesting that this is a way of organizing the facts which may prove more useful in enabling us to understand how the child learns to walk about normally.

But, secondly, even though we adopt this idea of two lines of development going on together, we are still assuming that the phases are related to each other in the causal manner which we have already described. After all, anybody who has watched a baby going through these stages can tell that he is 'learning' to walk, and that it is a skill which comes with practice. But is this really so? Certainly there are cases where the *innate growth pattern* produces a sequence of phenomena which are indistinguishable from the sort of causal sequence we have been discussing – indistinguishable, that is, if we rely on observation alone, unsupported by experiment. In the sort of case I have in mind, it seems quite clear to the observer that learning and practice are going on, that you have to do A before you can do B; but this does not fit the facts.

This is perhaps best seen in the case of experiments carried out on the development of animals. Take a bird learning to fly, for instance. If you observe this, you will see that it goes through three phases. Firstly, it makes random movements with its wings which seem to have little to do with flying. We could perhaps regard this as being an experimental phase similar to the stage of phonemes in language development; the fledgeling is getting to know where its wings are, and what it can do with them. Secondly, it makes fluttering motions which we might regard as incipient flying. Thirdly, it makes short uncertain flights during which it

appears to be just able to stay airborne. Finally, there comes a day
when it is able to fly with confidence. A very clear example, you
may say, of the sort of phase sequence we are discussing. But one
psychologist tried the experiment of confining the wings of a
pigeon in a kind of tube which prevented any kind of practice
movement. He watched a second pigeon from the same clutch of
eggs go through the kind of pattern of phases described above, and
when this bird was ably to fly with confidence, he released the
experimental pigeon from its confinement. It flew away as strongly
as the other bird.

We call this type of growth *maturation*. That is, development
which is due to the unfolding of the innate physiological properties of the animal. It is important to remember that the
phenomena produced by maturation may resemble very closely
the kind of model we have been discussing in which development
takes place through a causal sequence of phases. But, of course,
in cases of maturation, the phase sequence model does not work:
you can, as it were, get to the attic without walking up the stairs.

Of course, we cannot put babies in tubes to confine their limbs
for experimental purposes, but one or two experiments have been
done which seem to show that there are maturation effects at
work in human infants. Climbing stairs, for instance, is an activity
which appears to be learned through practice. But when a
psychologist carried out an experiment with identical twins,
allowing one, and only one, to gain practice by playing on a stair-
case every day, he found that there was little difference in the
twins' actual ability to cope with stairs at the end of the experiment.

Returning to the child learning to walk: which is the best model
to use? A single sequence of phases, two parallel lines of development, or the by-products of a maturation process? Perhaps I can
leave this as an exercise for the reader to carry out if he wishes to
follow up the subject and look at some of the references given at
the end of the book.

We have now seen that there are three patterns discussed so far between which we may choose when we are talking about developmental phases: a simple causal succession of phases; two or more chains of phases existing in parallel; a chain of phases which are not directly connected with each other as far as cause is concerned, but which arise from different levels of the maturation process. There is a fourth possibility.

To illustrate this, let us look at the child's moral development. In the past, a number of writers have described a small number of phases in the child's orientation to right and wrong. The following account is a generalized version, drawing on all of them.

Phase I: Pre-moral behaviour

The very young child has no idea of right and wrong, nor has he any idea of postponing gratifications; or indeed of imposing any kind of control over his desires. If a baby is hungry, he wants feeding *now*, with whatever food is available, no matter to whom it belongs. He has no concept of whether it belongs to anyone else, or whether he is entitled to it, or whether it might be good for his character to exercise a little self-control – the only criterion for accepting or rejecting it is nice or nasty.

Phase II: Expediency

Now we come to a stage where the toddler has learned that if he does certain things he is likely to get a reward (sweets or a cuddle, or told he's a good boy), and if he does other things, there are unpleasant consequences. Although this is not exactly what we mean by moral behaviour, we do at least now have the possibility of control. Situations are weighed up in terms of the pleasantness of the likely consequences, and the child accordingly decides that it is expedient to do good things and inexpedient to do forbidden ones. We are not arguing, of course, that he always makes his decision along these lines. He may have a poor memory for some things. He may want so badly to do others that his desire pushes the thought of possible punishments out of his mind. What we are saying is that, when he does stop to weigh up an action, it is likely to be on this naïvely expedient basis.

Phase III: Authoritarian

The wishes of his parents gradually become formalized, so that he decides what his conduct should be on an authoritarian basis. That is to say that what Daddy says is in itself a sufficient reason for doing or not doing something, regardless of the consequences. He no longer, in other words, has to have a reward to behave himself, but good behaviour tends to be equated with obedience and disobedience.

Phase IV: Intuitive morality

The parents' attitudes and judgements become incorporated into the child's own personality. He no longer works out what is right and wrong, either in terms of expediency or parental wishes, but simply 'knows' that you mustn't do certain things. Different psychologists have various views on just how this comes about, but this discussion should be followed up in the references given at the end; it is not directly relevant to our argument at this point.

Phase V: Conformity judgements

When the child goes to school, he finds himself in a society of people of his own age and status. As his social awareness grows, he comes to accept the norms of the group in which he is taking part as a basis for making moral judgements.

Phase VI: Altruistic morality

At the time of adolescence, according to many writers, we see the emergence of a kind of moral thinking which is based upon working out the consequences of particular kinds of action for other people, or for society as a whole.

If you look through the literature on this subject, you will see that many writers describe a phase pattern of this sort. The evidence is not always unambiguous, and you will find some disagreement as to the exact order in which some of the middle phases make their appearance. But the general picture is roughly the same.

When faced with a list of six phases like this, it is very easy to assume that they fall into a simple sequence of successive phases. This is particularly so in the present case, for in order to move into any phase which involves a control of the natural inclinations, the child must move out of Phase I. So far, so good – to get off the ground floor, he's got to go upstairs. But does it really work after this point?

In order to fit the model to our actual observations, we must maintain that, when a child starts valuing obedience for its own sake, he no longer bothers about expediency at all; that when he internalizes his parents' judgements, he abandons the first two. A moment's thought will show that this is not really the case: we can not view development of this kind in terms of a model of someone walking up to the attic.

In fact, with the exception of the first phase, as we have already mentioned, it seems truer to say that the phases of moral development stay with us, to some extent at least, for the rest of our lives. Obedience to parents becomes transferred to teachers and to the idea of authority in general; the idea of conscience is an important one for most of us. Don't we all have feelings that there are certain things which we know intuitively to be wrong? Similarly, because we make judgements on an altruistic basis, it does not follow that we necessarily abandon, on all occasions, considerations of what is expedient, or what the Joneses do.

It would seem then that what we are dealing with here is a fourth kind of developmental pattern, which we may call a sequence of *cumulative* phases. That is, the phases make their first appearance in an orderly sequence, as already described, but they are added to those existing already, so that rather than passing from one form of judgement to another, the child increases his repertoire of behaviour in proportion to his age.

One final point. If you look through the examples given in this chapter, you will see that, examining the sequences from a slightly different point of view, they illustrate the principles of development discussed in an earlier chapter. The tendency towards greater complexity, discrimination and specialization of function is apparent in the child's use of language just as much as in the development of his ability to get about. It is apparent, too, in his moral development – particularly if we adopt a cumulative model.

As an exercise, you may wish to apply the remaining principles, and work out exactly how they apply.

seven

Needs and Goals

ANOTHER way of looking at the child's development is to think of how his needs differ as he grows up. This approach does not exclude the possibility of thinking at the same time in terms of phase sequences.

The idea of needs, and the degree to which they are met by the environment, enables us to account for many aspects of development, particularly those connected with personality. We may think of the very young infant, for instance, as needing security. By this we mean emotional security and a warm continuous relationship. If this need is not met, there can be long-standing damage in many aspects of the child's personality. Children who have been deprived of this primary relationship tend to grow up with a particular impairment of personality; they lack the ability to relate emotionally to other people; they seem to be impaired in some way in their sense of self; they tend to be delinquent.

Another way of putting this is to think in terms of developmental goals. The developmental goal of the first phase of life is to begin to define a sense of self. That is, to learn to separate me from not me, the self from the environment, and to begin to relate this self both perceptually and emotionally to the outside world, which consists not only of the objects which the infant begins to perceive and differentiate around him, but also the people in his life, with whom he begins to form emotional relationships. It is in terms of the primary emotional relationship (which is usually, of course, with the baby's mother) that this sense of self is worked out. You see, then, why in this chapter, the idea of needs and goals is presented as one. It is not really possible to separate these two ideas from each other. They are simply different ways of looking at the same thing. The infant's developmental goal is to define himself in terms of the relationship with his mother. In order to achieve this, he needs a warm continuous relationship.

The toddler's developmental goals are the formation of the bases for future intellectual tools; the beginning of formation of concepts to do with space and time; the foundations, too, of social skills, learning how to get on with other people; and the beginnings of psychological skills to do with his personality and his behaviour, such as self-control. He achieves these goals through exploration and manipulation of his environment, which has been rapidly expanded through his having learnt to walk. His *needs* at this time are for continuing security so that he will have sufficient confidence to move out from the protective relationship with his mother in order to carry out these explorations. He needs, too, the opportunity to play and come in contact with other children.

In the middle years of childhood, the years spent in the primary school and ending with the onset of adolescence, the developmental goals are concerned with the acquisition of a large number of skills. Some of these are physical; the child needs to build up the co-ordination of his muscles, and you will have noticed how many of the activities preferred by children in this age group serve directly the achievement of this goal. The primary school child loves to do tricks; he stands on his hands, he carries out all sorts of stunts on a bicycle; he climbs trees, and so on. Some of the goals are intellectual. In school, he still seems to be working with very rudimentary skills, but this period is the one in which the acquisition of knowledge and academic skills proceeds at its fastest rate. The goals may be social; the child has moved out for the first time into a larger society and is learning how to deal with people of various age groups who are outside the family. (Unless he is lucky enough to have been to a play centre before going to school.)

Adolescence is another developmental phase with its own characteristic goals. These tasks are concerned with the establishment of an adult personal identity and with seeing that one has adult skills and competences. The adolescent has to come to grips with considerable changes in his perception of himself. These are brought about at one level by sheer changes in actual size and strength, and at another level by physical maturation, so that the adolescent has to take account of new emotional urges, not all of them directly sexual. This reappraisal of his image of himself is paralleled by changes in his perception of other people.

The idea of needs and goals brings us to the interesting question of critical periods. We have seen in an earlier chapter that certain processes of growth may be viewed as a sequence which has to be gone through in a particular order. We can now also view such a sequence as a series of consecutive sets of needs to be met, or goals to be achieved. If the sequence is truly consecutive and has some kind of causal link between the various steps, it follows that failure to achieve the first set of goals, or, if you like, failure of the environment to meet the first set of needs, necessarily results in a failure to move on to the next and subsequent levels. You will remember that, in discussing this kind of model, we talked about the need to pass through all the floors of a building before getting to the attic. Learning to talk was quoted as an example where this model holds good: failure to master the morphemes of a language will prevent the child from going on to build words. In other words, he has to grasp the fact that sound units of a language are things that have meanings before he can go any further. This grasp can be regarded as one of the developmental goals of the period; alternatively, we can say that he needs verbal stimulation – plenty of people around, talking to him, for this stage of his language development.

We have already spoken of the part played by maturation. It may be that this has another part to play. The child's innate physical and nervous organization might be such at particular periods that it is particularly suited to the fulfilment of a particular goal. If this period goes by without achieving that goal, his level of maturation may be changed, so that he is no longer capable of doing it at all.

Let us look at a few examples of how this process takes place. As is often the case, animals, with their comparatively simple psychological organization, provide a very clear example.

The Austrian psychologist, Konrad Lorenz, has carried out a lot of interesting work with geese. One of the developmental tasks of a young gosling is to learn, as it were, that it is a goose. I do not mean that it knows this, as human beings do; it is simply a convenient way of saying that it needs to learn to behave in a goose-like fashion towards other geese as it grows up. While it is young, it needs to follow the mother goose and not some other animal (say, a fox). When it is adult, it needs to follow the flight leader. It has to select a female goose for mating, and not some other species of bird.

This, you might think, all comes about through the operation of instinct, but it seems that this is not so. In order for these goals to be achieved, the image of a goose has to be 'imprinted' on the gosling's perceptions soon after it emerges from the shell. Its nervous organization appears to be ready for this imprinting for only a limited period; if it fails to take place, or if the wrong object is imprinted, then the bird's perceptions are radically altered for the rest of its life. If the bird is raised in an incubator and sees, during this critical period, a human being instead of another goose, the image of a human being is imprinted. Thus, Lorenz was able to ride about the Austrian country lanes on a bicycle with an arrowhead formation of adult geese flying behind him. There is also the very sad account of a drake which had imprinted the image of the motorboat belonging to the staff of the bird sanctuary, since the boat came across to its island to feed it every day. When spring came around, the drake would swim up and down near the motorboat, carrying out all its courtship displays, a pathetic spectacle of unrequited love.

Now we are not saying that the human baby is subject to an imprinting process like that described above: the conclusion to be drawn is a rather more general one. The gosling has a particular developmental goal, namely to learn, as it were, what species it belongs to; its nervous organization is such that there is a definite and limited period of time during which it is properly adapting to carry out this task. Its needs, during this time, include the sight of adult geese. If it learns wrongly during this period, it has lost its chance of correct learning for the rest of its life. When we talk about critical periods in human development, this is the sort of thing we have in mind.

To return to the example that was given at the beginning of this chapter: the very young infant, we saw, had the developmental goal of defining himself as an entity separate from the environment. Many psychologists have argued that the achievement of this goal represents not just a phase pattern, such as we discussed in the last chapter, but an activity which must be carried out in a critical period, lasting in this case for the first few years of life. If the child fails to achieve this during this period, he makes a bad adjustment, which, if he passes on out of the critical period, cannot be relearnt. This is the point behind much of the literature about maternal deprivation.

Of course, there are very severe ethical limits on the sort of experimental work that should be carried out with children. Usually, psychologists working in this field have to rely on observation instead. Although common sense would seem to suggest that observation is a reliable way of finding out how children develop, there are a number of difficulties, particularly when (as is the case with talk about needs and goals) we are thinking about cause and effect.

The difficulty is something like this. The observer sees that most children are loved by their mothers, and that this is expressed by the child being picked up, fondled and spoken to. By and large, children who have this experience seem to avoid certain disturbances in their personality development in later years. On the other hand, children who have been, for example, orphaned, are deprived not only of the emotional relationship, but also of the actual expression of it as well. These children, it has been seen, tend very often to grow up to be delinquent and lacking in the capacity for affection. It is argued on the basis of such observations that the child has an emotional need (connected in the way already described with the developmental goals of the period) which, if not met, leads to certain disorders. But the difficulty is that in real life situations everything is more complicated; there are many things going on at once. Are we justified in separating the emotional relationship from its manifestations? Certainly, many psychologists would argue that the child's needs can best be described in terms of sensory stimulation. This is associated with the mother's presence, because, generally speaking, the mother is biologically much more strongly motivated towards patiently and consistently carrying out the right sort of action than is any substitute.

Thus we have one of the disagreements between experts which the newcomer to the field finds so perplexing. The disagreement, however, though fundamental, is not so serious as far as practical application is concerned as might appear at first sight, since the application of either model will lead to the same behaviour on the part of the mother (who, in any case, is more likely to be responding to her own feelings of what she enjoys doing than to what it says in psychology textbooks).

Another example which is frequently cited in support of the idea of critical periods is the task of learning to speak. We have already seen that this may be viewed as a simple pattern of consecutive phases, in which each stage must be effectively accomplished before the child can move on to the next one. It could well be that the earliest phases must be carried out in the first few years of life. Occasionally, children have been found who, through extraordinary circumstances, have been isolated from their kind for the first few years of life, and who have had no opportunity to learn human speech. In India, some years ago, two children were discovered who had apparently spent their lives among wolves. Although they were taken into care, and although attempts were made to 'humanize' them, endeavours to teach them to speak met with very little success. Looking at an example nearer to our everyday experience, we find that fluency in foreign languages is acquired more easily in proportion to the earliness of the age at which the individual begins. Very young children do not 'learn'

French in the sense of getting to know grammatical rules and lists of irregular verbs, they just pick it up in a way which will become impossible as they get older. This example is particularly important, since it may serve as an illustration for one way in which we might modify the idea of a critical period.

One criticism of the critical period concept is that it can lead to an unduly pessimistic or fatalistic attitude on the part of people who are concerned with bringing up children. If something should have been learnt at a particular age, and that age has gone by, then there is nothing we can do about it; we must simply accept the child's limitations. Now, in so far as psychology or child development attempts to be a scientific study, such considerations are not relevant to our attempts at building theories. If it is true that this is how a child works, then it is our duty to report this, irrespective of the consequences. But we have already argued that the word 'true' can be very misleading in this sort of context, and we must be very sure about the irreversibility of the effects before we subscribe to a theory whose application is going to help to ensure that they *are* irreversible. In addition, the higher you go up the evolutionary ladder, the more you find that behaviour becomes flexible in the sense that it is less dependent on innate physiological mechanisms. Human beings are very much more behaviourally flexible organisms than geese. We therefore should not be surprised to discover that there is a much smaller degree of irreversibility in human beings.

This should not lead us to abandon entirely the idea of the critical period. There is plenty of evidence, as we have seen, that something of this kind happens. But it may lead us to modify it, so that it is less final and puts less emphasis on whether the effects of deprivations are irreversible.

Let us look again at the example of language learning. Are we arguing that, once the initial period of easy acquisition of language has gone by, the individual will never learn to speak, or never learn to speak another language? Obviously, this is not true. People do learn foreign languages at all kinds of ages, profoundly deaf children can make, with the right teaching, progress in language, even when it has been left rather late. In these cases, however, the task is accomplished only with much more difficulty, and by the use of quite different methods of learning.

So, in a sense, the idea of the critical period remains true. If we are talking about 'picking up' a language efficiently, this can only be done easily at a particular point in development, lasting for a few years. But, because the human being is flexible, language can be acquired by other means after this period has gone by. (We might suggest in passing that one of the difficulties with the 'wolf children' was the extreme paucity of their background, which robbed them of these other means, too.)

For practical purposes, then, we might replace the idea of a critical period with that of an *optimal period*; that is, a time during which a developmental goal can be achieved more easily, quickly, naturally, and with the minimum expenditure of effort.

PART TWO

THREE APPROACHES TO DEVELOPMENT

The following chapters will give some idea of the way different psychologists, all of them concerned with development, go about organizing their data into a coherent theory. You will see, too, how the concepts introduced in the preceding section, make their appearance in an actual working context.

eight

Piaget – Phases in Intellectual and Conceptual Development

In the introductory chapter, I described an experiment concerned with the child's idea of volume, and another in the same section in which the child's idea of family relationships was explored by means of question and answer. These experiments were carried out in the Institute of Educational Sciences at Geneva, under the supervision of Professor Jean Piaget, and they are typical of the type of observation on which Piaget's theory of development is based. Perhaps I can refresh your memory by giving you two more examples which will show how the child's thinking processes are investigated by means of very simple, and yet subtle, questions.

A child of five years is shown two sticks, arranged under each other. He is asked whether they are the same size, and of course he agrees that they are. Now, *while he is watching*, one of the sticks is moved to one side, so that its end sticks out beyond that of the other, and he is again asked whether the two sticks are the same length. Although he has watched the operation, the five-year-old child says that they are not equal, and usually picks on the top one as being the longer of the two. If this simple experiment is repeated with an eight-year-old child, he will assert that the two sticks are still the same length – 'You can't change their length by moving them about'.

An eleven-year-old boy is talking to an interviewer. The interviewer asks, 'Are there more ducks or more birds?'

'The ducks are birds as well.'

'Well then?'

'There are more birds.'

. . . 'Suppose that one hunter wants to shoot all the ducks, and another wants to shoot all the birds. Would there be more left after killing all the ducks, or all the birds?'

'When I kill all the birds.'

'Why?'

'If one kills all the ducks and all the birds, the ducks are birds as well.'

The conversation is about the child's ability to put things into classifications and to understand the nature of classifications of this sort. I will leave the reader to work out what is the error which the child in the interview is making.

Piaget is one of the most influential psychologists working at the present time. His background includes biology and philosophy, as well as psychology. From his biological studies comes his conviction that development takes place in as orderly a fashion in the mental and behavioural sphere as in the physical; from philosophy comes his interest in the development of the cognitive aspects of the growing child; that is those aspects which are concerned mainly with thought.

In particular, Piaget's theories have been mainly concerned with the child's perceptions of the world around him, and with the concepts which he forms about it. Although this may seem, by comparison with some of the personality theories we are looking at in this book, an unduly restricted approach, you will see that a study of this kind tells us a great deal about the child's general development, since his perceptions of, and concepts about, the world are bound to include social as well as purely intellectual matters.

The main principles underlying Piaget's idea of development are not dissimilar from some of the principles of development described above in an earlier chapter. We can summarize them under the following headings:

(i) All development is continuous and proceeds through generalization and differentiation.

In spite of this continuity, development goes through a definite and orderly sequence of phases, which may differ from each other, not merely in quantity, but also in kind.

(ii) The apparent paradox implied by the above two principles is resolved by saying that each phase of development has its roots in the one before, and also provides a necessary basis for the building of the next one. Piaget's view of development is therefore essentially one of *consecutive* phases.

As you might expect from someone who has been working at the subject consistently for so many years (since about 1924), and who has published so formidable a volume of works (thirty-three in one bibliography), the formulation of the theory varies from time to time, according to the particular aspect of development which is being discussed. The description given below is of the version which is most generally applicable, and which is most widely associated with Piaget's name.

The child's development is seen as falling into five phases: the sensori-motor phase; the pre-conceptual phase; the phase of intuitive thought; the phase of concrete operations; and the phase of formal operations. These names may seem somewhat intimidating at first sight, but they will be explained below, and it is hoped that their appropriateness will become apparent.

The Sensori-motor Phase

This phase extends over approximately the first twenty-four months from birth. The term sensori-motor indicates that the child is mainly concerned at this time with the sensations conveyed to him through his nervous system, and with the development of motor activities; that is the powers of movement. The main developmental tasks of this phase are to learn to co-ordinate his actions (motor activities) and his perceptions of himself and the world (sensory activities) into some sort of whole.

In the first instance, the baby is assailed by unco-ordinated sensory experiences which appear to have little pattern and little reference to anything in the environment or in himself. Similarly, the movements he makes are at random, or are purely reflex actions; he has little, if any, voluntary control over them.

The process by which these disconnected experiences are co-ordinated is of such importance that Piaget subdivides this phase into six substages. A brief summary such as this is not the place for an account of such refinement, and I shall instead simply give the direction of growth and its main characteristics.

As I have said, the earliest type of action is connected with reflexes which are repeated and which tend to form habits. At this time, the infant is in an autistic phase. That is, he responds to his environment entirely according to his own needs, which of course at this stage are purely physical. Presently, reflex actions are slowly replaced by voluntary activity. This is partly dependent on maturation. In their first manifestations, voluntary activities appear when the infant is able to repeat on purpose an action which it has formerly carried out by accident or as a reflex action. For instance, a baby is lying in its pram. A rattle is hanging on a string from the pram hood, where the baby can see it. He makes a random movement, stretching his legs and rolling about, to find a more comfortable position. This causes the rattle to dance about. It catches the baby's eye. He is pleased and laughs at it. In the earliest phase he accepts this experience passively. As he moves into the next stage, he is able to wriggle on purpose, so as to make the rattle move.

By the end of the first year, such activities have become organized to the extent that the child is able to reach for an object which has been obscured. Piaget charted these phases by watching his own children develop. At six months, if he offered the baby a box, but had some obstacle in the way, the baby tried to get round the obstacle, but had no idea of moving it. By the time he was eight months old, however, the baby would hit at the top of a soft cushion so as to lower it and reach his toy. We are seeing, in other words, the beginnings of *instrumental* behaviour.

By the time he is two years old, the sensory and motor experiences are organized into some sort of a whole, and the child is able to begin to use them to solve problems. The problems used in the research are of a very simple kind, such as putting a watch-chain into a match-box which is only opened half an inch. Whereas the younger child can be observed to make seventeen or eighteen attempts consecutively, during the course of which he does not find the solution until the sixteenth attempt, and forgets it again for the eighteenth, the slightly older child takes only four attempts to realize that it can best be managed by rolling the chain up into a little ball.

Also at this stage the child is beginning to organize some idea of space. One object may go behind another. For the very young child, it has disappeared, it is lost. The child who is at the end of the sensori-motor stage can look behind the obstruction to find the missing object, and can even walk round obstructions when this involves turning his back on the lost object.

Pre-conceptual Phase: two to four years old
Whereas the last phase was described as autistic, this one is labelled ego-centric. The child's world is still self-centred, but there is an advance in that there is now a self to be at the centre of the world, instead of simply a succession of sensations and demands. The sensory and motor experiences have been organized into the beginnings of an ego.

The main activity of the pre-conceptual child is play, which occupies most of his waking time. It is through play that the child begins to gather information about his environment so that this can be organized at a later stage, just as he has previously organized his sensory and motor experience. Language, too, develops quickly at this stage, but is used entirely in an ego-centric way. For example, the statement 'Soup is hot' tends to mean to the child that his own soup is hot and will burn *his* mouth. It is only later that this becomes a statement that might be applicable to all hot soups, and all mouths.

The child's experiences in play and in his relationships with other people enable him to organize such concepts as space and spatial relationships, but judgements about such things are still at an entirely subjective level. You will remember the experiment in which a child was asked which glass contained the greater amount of liquid. Pre-conceptual children behave in everyday life in the way seen in the research. They will choose a small glass filled to the rim with milk in preference to a glass twice as big which is only three-quarters full. He has an idea of fullness which is not connected to objective ideas of volume.

Phase of Intuitive Thought

This phase is represented by the four- to seven-year-old. The child is beginning to come into contact with others, particularly when he goes to school. This tends to reduce ego-centricity. He must begin to coordinate his ego-centric version of the world with the real world around him. During this phase, he begins to act in consistent patterns, behaving similarly to elders. He exhibits the first real beginnings of thinking.

That it is *real* thinking in one sense is shown by the fact that he now verbalizes his thoughts, though he frequently has to do this out loud. His thinking, however, does not correspond with reasoning as adults would understand it, and he can only entertain one idea at a time.

A simple experiment demonstrates this. A child is given two identical sets of counters. They are arranged in two parallel lines close together. The child is able to tell the experimenter that the quantity is the same in each case. While the child is watching, the rows are rearranged into two piles, equal in number but spread to occupy unequal areas. The child will now say that the most spread out heap contains more buttons than the other one. He cannot hold the concept of a constant quantity over into a new situation.

The child's knowledge tends to be specific and limited in a variety of concepts, such as his use of language. Frequently, he knows which is his right arm and which his left, but has no concept of right or left in the general sense. Similarly, the person who comes in first in a race is not only the winner, but also the fastest runner, regardless of the different distances that might have been imposed by a handicapping system. There is, you will see, some attempt at reasoning, which is a step forward, but, as we have stated, it is not adult reasoning.

Another example is given by the child's learning of numbers. Most parents teach their children to count before they go to school. It does not follow that they have any concept of what the numbers really mean. A child who can count up to ten is still likely to judge the number of counters on the basis of their appearance rather than on the basis of their numerical quantity.

Another characteristic of this phase is its animism. That is, everything which impinges on him is seen as being alive. A three-year-old is likely to have bumped her head on a naughty table, or tripped over a wicked mat. At the beginning of the phase, this animism is applied to everything. By the end of it, life is only attributed to things which seem to be able to move of their own volition, whether they be motor-cars or clouds moving across the sky.

The Phase of Concrete Operations

This phase occupies the remaining time before adolescence. The child is beginning to be capable of a new level of thought that Piaget calls operational thought. That is, for the first time he is able to order experience into an organized whole. However, for this age group, we are limited to concrete operations, which means that mental operations cannot be carried out unless the child can directly perceive the logic of the situation.

In the example of the two rows of counters, the child in this phase is able to see that the quantities are constant and cannot be changed simply by altering the positions of the objects, but he cannot generalize about this; he cannot conceptualize so as to make a rule about constancy of quantities without having actual counters, or their equivalent in terms of which he can work it out.

The Phase of Formal Operations

From about the age of twelve, the child becomes able to use symbolism in a general way and to think about abstract principles.

The characteristics of this phase are really implied by what has been said before.

We might summarize Piaget's system of phases in terms of the following developmental tasks :

1. To co-ordinate sensory and motor impressions, exploring *himself*, as it were to provide a frame of reference in the world in which he finds himself.
2. To explore his world so that he begins to place himself in relation to it.
3. To begin to use symbols with which he can describe the world.
4. To begin to understand the workings of the world, without however understanding the general principles underlying it.
5. To understand logical and abstract principles.

nine

Erikson – A Psychology of Needs and Goals

IN THE last chapter, we examined a developmental scheme which grouped the child's intellectual growth into a number of phases. These phases, we saw, led to developmental tasks being postulated. In Erikson's scheme, the emphasis is reversed: a number of developmental goals or tasks are distinguished, and these lead to the formulation of a number of distinct stages of development.

Erikson's work is psychoanalytic in its bias. This means that a great deal of the material on which it is based is derived from clinical observation and case history rather than from experiment. There is, however, in his work a great deal of reference to anthropological studies of children in various cultures, ranging from the Sioux Indians to twentieth-century Germany and Russia.

This scheme of development postulates eight phases: infancy; early childhood; play age; school age; adolescence; young adulthood; adulthood; mature age. Each of these periods is characterized by its own developmental task. Each task has two opposed solutions, and the one chosen influences the child's development for the rest of his life. This chapter will give a brief explanation of these phases and developmental tasks. You may remember that, in an earlier chapter, I mentioned the jibe that developmental psychologists lose interest in the child as soon as it becomes an adult. This certainly does not apply to Erikson, who, almost alone among the students of development, extends his scheme into adulthood and maturity. For reasons of space, however, we shall

restrict ourselves to the first five phases – infancy to adolescence,
these being the stages which are directly comparable with other
developmental schemes discussed here.

Phase I. Infancy: Trust versus Mistrust
On the satisfactory completion of the developmental task of this
phase rests all later development. This task is the acquisition of a
sense of basic trust. To achieve this, the child needs physical com-
fort and a minimum of fear and uncertainty.

The alternative solutions are simple. He can come to regard the
environment as a place in which he can exist with confidence, or
as something threatening, something to be mistrusted. The solution chosen is important for all future learning. A sense of basic
trust enables the child to move on to new experiences, to later
phases and to other developmental tasks; basic mistrust will
hamper his development, since he will not move on to other
activities willingly or easily.

Turning to the detailed tasks of the period, these are centred
upon body functions. The child has to breathe, feed, sleep, and so
on, and these are his primary concerns. The infant is therefore
totally egocentric.

Social and emotional development have, however, their roots
in this period. The child is taking part in a primitive relationship
with his mother. We have seen, in an earlier chapter, how other
psychologists have described the way in which this relationship
has its effect on later character development. It is also, of course,
a *social* relationship of a very primitive kind, and is thus the
foundation of future social development. The establishment of a
satisfactory relationship is one of the important developmental
tasks of the period.

Phase II. Early Childhood: Autonomy versus Shame and Doubt
This phase lasts from about eighteen months to four years. During
this period, the child's world changes very rapidly. On the one
hand, there is a dramatic maturation, which results in the accomplishment of the simple, but necessary, physical skills, like walk-

ing, climbing, reaching things, all of which help to expand his effective environment. He is also likely to experience for the first time attempts to train him in various directions – control over eating habits, over temper, and, of course, toilet training, which can loom very large to both child and mother.

The principal developmental goal of this period is the acquisition of a sense of autonomy. That is, the child must move on from a position of being dependent on the adult world for everything to a stage where he sees himself as an independent entity, capable of carrying out at least some activities on his own. As an infant, he was dependent on the adult world for every mouthful of food, for being picked up and moved about, or put down to sleep, for being given toys and rattles which he could not reach. Now he must learn to do many of these things for himself.

However, the adult world sets limits upon these independent activities. The child can explore the house, but must not go too near the fire; he can play in the garden, but must not go through the gate on to the road. Of course, he cannot know what these limits are until he runs up against them. Here we have the possibility of conflict. The child's striving for autonomy expresses itself in experiment and self-assertion, which from time to time brings him into conflict with his parents. Such conflict may result in the emergence of feelings of doubt about his capacity, and about his own autonomy. Autonomy and doubt are the two antithetical solutions to the typical problem of early childhood, and again the solution chosen is going to affect all departments of a child's later development.

The child's need at this period is for sympathetic support and encouragement in his exploration of the world, so that his emerging autonomy will be fostered, and so that the necessary conflicts with adult restrictions do not thrust him into shame and doubt.

In terms of actual behaviour, we see this development in the child's determination to do things on his own, and in the indignant repudiation of attempts to feed him, to hold his hand when he's walking somewhere, to dress him, to open the door for him. The *Leitmotiv* of this period is, 'Me do it'.

To meet the developmental needs of this phase, the mother needs to be able to shift her attitude dramatically. Whereas only a few months previously, her willingness to see to *all* his needs was a necessary means of giving the child a sense of basic trust, she must now be able to stand back when necessary, and to let the child move out from this position to experiment with his own capacities.

Phase III. Play Age: Initiative versus Guilt

The third phase comprises the remaining pre-school years. It is characterized by the great importance which playing has for children at these ages. Playing, of course, is, for young children, a very serious matter. It consists, to a large degree of acting various roles from the adult world, and it is at this age that the behaviour of boys and girls begins to diverge, each becoming characterized by its own social norm.

The developmental task of the period, and its antithesis, are extensions of the one that has gone before. The child wants to assume yet more responsibility for himself, but this responsibility is now extended to include things outside himself, such as his toys, and sometimes pets, or younger brothers or sisters. In the course of his play, he is testing out his abilities and skills and capacities.

Through these activities, he develops the sense of initiative. His world is expanding and his wider activities are beginning to pull him away from the dependent relationship he has had with his parents. This is the origin of the sense of guilt which will tend to operate in the other direction. He tends sometimes to go too far in his movement towards independence, but if he gives in to his feelings of guilt, he may develop a passive state of mind in which his explorations are likely to be curtailed.

If this period is characterized by initiative in an expanding world, the child's needs can be summed up as the provision of an environment which really is expanding. He needs to meet other children, and to play with them. A nursery school, a play centre or a kindergarten will provide an enriched environment in which his initiative can develop. Again, the parents must be capable of standing back and letting the child grow.

Phase IV. School Age: Industry versus Inferiority
This period coincides mainly with the years in the primary school. The child is developing in a number of directions and his progress is rapid – if you watch it closely, it frequently seems bewilderingly so. He is developing a variety of physical skills; he is learning the basis of any future academic attainment he may achieve. He is learning about the nature of society and acquiring all the social skills necessary for getting on with people.

From this array, Erikson selects as the major theme of the period the developmental task of acquiring a sense of industry. The other side of the coin is the possible acquisition of a sense of inferiority. The child in school is brought into contact with a wider world of adults. He sees how much more they know than he does, how many more things they can do that he cannot: he sees, in short, that he is a child, and this may bring about undue feelings of inferiority. By this, we do not mean that to avoid the difficulty the child must see himself as knowing as much, or being able to do as much, as adults; this would simply be delusion. What we mean is that the child's perception of his incompleteness and present inferiority should not lead him to a defeatist attitude in which he feels that there is just too much to do, too much to learn; that there is no point in trying, and that he might just as well relax into an earlier, more comfortable, phase. To overcome these fears of inferiority, the child needs to develop a sense of industry, a determination to succeed with what he is doing. He experiments with everything from physical skills to school work and symbolic thought.

In discussing patterns of growth, we talked about asynchronous development. This is particularly evident during this period, since physical maturation slows down and is restricted to a fairly steady increase in height and weight, which is proportionally much slower than in both the preceding and following periods.

In many societies, the child takes part for the first time in a 'society of childhood'. This is a genuine social organization of children of about the same age. This is the time when the child tries out his social skills, and learns new ones, entirely without adult supervision.

Erikson attaches great importance to this period as a whole, and says that many of the individual's later attitudes towards work can be traced to the degree of a successful sense of industry gained during this phase.

Phase V. Adolescence: Identity versus Identity Diffusion

Adolescence is a time of quite dramatic acceleration in physical, emotional and social development, and brings the young person face to face with a whole lot of new problems to solve. The problem which Erikson selects as being the key question of the period is the acquisition of a sense of identity. That is, the person, in order to be able to move out successfully into the adult world, must know who he is, and what his capacities are. However, the adolescent is thinking mainly, as it were, in the future tense; not so much 'What am I?', but 'What can I do?' Of course, the potentialities are very wide, as are the loyalties and identifications carried over from earlier phases. So many are these demands that there is the danger of the adolescent's sense of identity being diffused over too large a field, so that he is not competent to behave consistently in the face of adult problems. Added to this, many of the skills of childhood are temporarily thrown out of co-ordination by the sudden spurt of growth. Even physical abilities which reach a fairly high peak by the pre-adolescent period may be replaced by a temporary clumsiness, which arises from the fact that the adolescent's feet, say, are not where they were in relation to his body six months ago. This kind of problem, too, may undermine his confidence and interfere with the development of his sense of identity.

We may sum up the problem by saying that the adolescent has to make a synthesis of past and future. He has to co-ordinate the skills and attitudes which have been built up in earlier periods, fit them together with his perception of himself now into a new adult type personality, and line these up with future goals to do with his job, marriage, and so on.

Erikson goes on to list seven different activities which are important for this phase, indicating the importance which he attaches to it. These are a need to build up a concept of time on a sufficient scale to see his life in perspective, instead of as it comes. The need to build up some degree of self-certainty. The need to experiment with various roles and to avoid negative identity, that is adopting a role for no better reason other than that it is the opposite of that which is approved of by his elders. He needs to bring his sense of industry to bear in a persistent way; that is, he needs to be able to work consistently towards a distant goal, rather than to be industrious about individual tasks as they come along. He needs to see himself as a male (or female). He must work out his attitudes to authority, and finally he must select a basic philosophy, ideology or religion.

ten

Ausubel – The Changing Status of the Child

This is a theory of development which is concerned principally with personality. In particular, personality is seen as something which is shaped by the social situation of the child, that is, the inter-relationships between him and the other people around him. For the most part, these are, particularly at the earliest age levels, members of his own family, but they become, of course, increasingly concerned with society as a whole. This concern with the social aspect of personality is reflected in Ausubel's terminology, which is sociological in tone. Of particular interest from our point of view is the use of a striking analogy – far removed from the idea of a 'straight', or 'true', causal explanation – to give us greater insight into the nature of certain developmental changes.

Ausubel describes the developmental process as falling into only three phases: infancy, childhood and adolescence; the latter, of course, leads on to a final phase of adulthood. Each of these phases has its own characteristic personality organization, and each of them is separated from the others by a period of drastic personality reorganization.

Phase I. Infancy: The Omnipotent Personality
The infant has an 'omnipotent' personality organization. Perhaps we ought to consider exactly what the author means by this term. He does not mean, of course, that the infant has delusions of omnipotence in the same way that an adult would if he were to,

say, become insane and believe to be God. As we have seen, the infant is not capable, either in terms of concept development, or even in terms of vocabulary, to formulate an abstract idea of this kind.

To try and imagine what the omnipotent personality is like, and how it comes about, consider what the world looks like to an infant. He is hungry and cries; people appear and feed him. He is uncomfortable, and people clean him and clothe him. Their only functions, as far as other people impinge on his senses, are to serve him. He is not yet capable of envisaging them as having an existence of their own away from him. He is the centre of his universe.

It is necessary that this should be so. The infant is not yet equipped to deal with hunger and loneliness and discomfort. He cannot deal with it in the physical sense, nor can he deal with the frustrations involved in not having his needs attended to by his world. If he is obliged to relinquish the omnipotent position too soon, this may lead to losses in security and self-esteem. We have seen in an earlier chapter how it may lead to serious disturbances of personality.

We have seen, too, how the other authors, whose work is discussed in this section, have regarded the earliest phases of development as characterized by ego-centricity. Ausubel's concept of the omnipotent personality of infancy is concerned with the same phenomena.

Of course, the omnipotent personality cannot be retained indefinitely. Parents begin to say 'No!'; the child himself begins to realize that, far from being omnipotent, there are very narrowly circumscribed limits set upon what he can do. He finds himself to be a very small child in a world of powerful and clever adults, who have purposes and functions unrelated to him. He realizes that he is not the centre of the universe.

Phase II. Childhood: The Satellite Personality

What are the implications of the child's relinquishing the omnipotence of childhood? We can illustrate some of them by means of an analogy with the development of our views of the place of the human race in the universe.

For many hundreds of years, men imagined the earth to be the centre of the universe. The sun and the moon were placed in the sky only to provide the earth with warmth and light. The human race was at the centre of things, and everything seemed to have been created for its benefit. When Copernicus discovered that the earth goes round the sun, this had a profoundly disturbing effect on people's thinking, because of its implication about man's importance in the universe. The idea was vigorously resisted by many, and most of those who accepted it were only able to do so by limiting the amount of displacement: the centre of the universe was at first displaced from the earth only as far as the sun, allowing us to keep ourselves at the centre, if only on a satellite basis.

For the infant, the revolution which follows upon the loss of the omnipotent personality is no less fundamental. We are accustomed to thinking about the problems faced by the adolescent; the problems of personality reorganization faced by the pre-school child are no less extensive.

Self-esteem must be preserved, but how can this be achieved? Our analogy suggests the answer. If the child cannot be the centre of the universe, then his parents are, and he can become their satellite. Hence the name for this phase: the satellite personality of childhood.

More prosaically, we can look at the same problems in the child's development in terms of his status, distinguishing between *primary status*, and *derived status*. Primary status is that which is due to the individual's own competence and attributes; derived status arises from the status of some other socially related persons.

The satellite personality of childhood is characterized by *derived* status, due mainly not to the child's own skills and attributes, but to those of his parents. You should note at this point that we are not talking only about the child's actual status, as viewed by society, but also of his perception of his own status.

His status is derived because he is economically dependent on his parents – I do not mean that they are the source of his pocket-money, but that they feed him, house him, clothe him, and so on. He is also emotionally dependent on his parents in all sorts of ways; he cannot usually cope with outside relationships without having at least the possibility of running back to his parents for support, sympathy or encouragement.

Of course, as time passes, he does begin to earn primary status gradually, usually in limited settings. In his own gang, his status is connected with how well he can wrestle, or whether he can ride a bicycle with no hands, or whatever is the approved activity of the group. This is almost entirely a reflexion of his own competence. Similarly in the classroom, his status is in part dependent on how good he is at reading or arithmetic. Outside the classroom, his ability at games may be important. I have spoken of 'he', but there are, of course, similar opportunities for limited primary status for a girl. Such opportunities, however, occur only gradually until the child becomes an adolescent.

Phase III. Adolescence: Achieving Primary Status

This brings us to the third phase in personality development, that of adolescence, which is perhaps best viewed as being a parallel to the earlier 'Copernican revolution' phase, rather than as being equivalent to either of the earlier personalities. Just as the omnipotent personality could not cope with the facts of the real world, so the satellite personality of childhood is inadequate to deal with the pressures which impinge upon the adolescent. A further revolution must take place.

The pressures on the adolescent are of various kinds. First, we have those which are the direct consequences of the physical changes associated with puberty. These, as we have seen, are of two types, concerned with physical size and physical maturation. Secondly, there are indirect consequences. There are changes in the adolescent's perception of himself, and there are changes in the attitudes of other people towards him. These attitudes often express conflict. Our expectations are often linked to our perception of the individual's size. He begins to assume adult proportions, and we begin to expect him to be an adult, without always having sufficient regard to the fact that the adolescent does not have an adult's quantity of experience. We are therefore pushing him, socially speaking, in the direction of becoming grown up. At the same time, we are in other respects unwilling to grant adult status – perhaps because, as parents or teachers, his progress may be felt to affect our own standing, so we are holding him back.

This conflict of adult attitude is particularly clear in the case of parents, who may want their children to progress and may take pride in their independence, while at the same time – regretting the loss of the intimacy and dependence of earlier stages – resenting the fact that the young person is now able to stand on his own feet. In our society, with its high valuation of youth and its horror of ageing, the conflict of attitude may have additional aspects, since the maturity of the child may be seen as evidence of the ageing of the parents.

Adolescence, therefore, is seen not as a simple drive towards maturity, but as a situation of conflict and ambivalence. This conflict derives partly from the world outside, but it exists, too, in the adolescent himself. He wants to move on and prove his adult competence. At the same time, he is reluctant to leave the cosy security of his familiar derived status. Thus we find, particularly in early adolescence, remarkable shifts from one attitude to another.

The developmental tasks of the adolescent are summed up by saying that he must assume primary status in spite of these conflicts and difficulties. In particular, he must (i) become emotionally independent of his parents: (ii) get to know his own skills and competences, so that he can be economically independent: (iii) come to have a sufficient degree of self-esteem to realize that these skills are of adult grade.

Adolescence, then, is a period of drastic and extensive revision of the personality.

Ausubel goes on to discuss the application of this theory to our own type of society. His discussion of the problems of adolescence is of particular interest.

Modern urban society is often held to be responsible for the disturbances in adolescent behaviour. Ausubel tries to provide us with an explanation of what is going wrong.

Modern urban society provides few genuine means by which the adolescent can feel that he is achieving primary status. Perhaps we can understand this statement better by looking at a few examples of societies in which such opportunities are provided.

In primitive societies, everyone is closer to the skills necessary for survival, and the adolescent, who is, after all, approaching the peak of his physical capacity, is able to play a genuine part in the life of the community, whether it be agricultural or based on hunting. The skills concerned are such that he can take a pride in them. Their contribution to the community can be seen as genuine, not only by him, but also by those around him.

In simple rural societies, the adolescent also has opportunities of this kind, fields in which he can demonstrate that he has adult status. Even if there are few decisions which he can take, he can be quite competent at genuine jobs, like milking and herding, and so on. There are also rural pastimes, such as shooting or fishing, at which he can equal or surpass the adult.

Even in complex industrial societies like ours, there are certain periods of national crisis or need, during which there is a primary role for the adolescent or very young adult. This perhaps is the reason, or at least part of it, why many people look back on wartime with such an astonishing nostalgia. There was a role for young people, a genuine need, and an opportunity for achievement of primary status which does not exist, except in more primitive societies. We are familiar with the role played by 'the few' in the Battle of Britain. Constant representation of these by ageing cinema and television stars tends to obscure the fact that most of them were in fact extremely young – in many cases late adolescents.

In more settled times, however, such opportunities are rare. The skills which the adolescent is acquiring are far removed, to his own and to anybody else's perception, from the realities of keeping the society going. Perhaps we cannot do without someone who is studying French, English and history, or filing tax records at the Inland Revenue all day, or pressing the button which puts the cap on the tomato ketchup, but these activities cannot always be seen as involving vital skills, or as making a positive contribution to society.

It is, of course, one thing to diagnose a failing, and quite another to say how it should be put right. Ausubel does in fact go on to discuss the practical implications, but these are beyond the scope of this book. Perhaps the reader might like to work some of them out for himself before comparing his conclusions with what Ausubel actually says.

eleven

Conclusion

THE THEORIES of development which were discussed briefly in
the second part of this book differ in a number of ways, but they
cannot be said to contradict each other. A number of common
elements, such as the egocentricity of infancy, can be traced in all
of them. Unfortunately, this does not seem to be true of all alternative developmental theories. We may often find that two
alternative explanations seem to be mutually exclusive. How are
we to deal with this situation when it occurs?

In the first chapter, I stressed the need for a degree of objectivity in this kind of work. This may lead to a further question.
Surely, if everyone were objective, there would be no room for
rival theories. And why bother to have theories at all? Why not
simply give a straight account of what we observe?

One difficulty is that the role of completely objective reporting
is rather limited. It would be possible to compile a list, for
example, of all of the activities connected with moving about
which are carried out by babies and which culminate in learning
to walk. It would be possible to arrange these in chronological
order. Such a list may be found in almost any textbook on child
development. But, by itself, it can tell us very little. Are these
various activities connected with each other in some way? Is it
necessary to do one before one can learn to do the next in the
list? Such questions can only be answered if the data is ordered
into some more structured form.

This is one of the principal functions of theory. It provides a
model which connects the various pieces of information in a
coherent manner, and which permits us to come to conclusions

about causal relationships. Of course, theories must fit in with various criteria. They must take into account, and be consistent with, all the known and relevant facts. They should do so by making as few hypotheses as possible. And, to be practical, they should point the way to some course of action. Theory is often decried by those who see it as the opposite of practice; in reality they are complementary, and theory is better regarded as being the precursor of practice. A theory of development is, too, likely to be a useful means of obtaining still further data about our subject. The process is the same as in other areas of scientific inquiry. We begin by assembling the data available: we construct a theory which appears to make sense of it, and then, as a final step, we make a prediction based on our theory. Such a prediction is tested by further observation or experiment. If our prediction proves to be correct, we have obtained additional data which tends to substantiate the theory itself. If not, then the theory must be modified or replaced.

But what of the situation where there are rival theories dealing with the same aspect of development? One of the main reasons why people become over-concerned about this sort of situation is that they tend to expect too much from the theory itself. There is a considerable danger that we may be tempted to regard explanations of this sort as being in some way objectively true. Now the area in which such apparent disagreements happen so often is the development of personality. One finds that personality traits like anxiety may be accounted for in terms of child rearing practices and resulting interpersonal relations at a very early age; or in terms of conditioned reflexes; or in terms of social learning, and so on. It is naïve to think that if one of these approaches is 'right', then the others must be 'wrong'. Each of them represents a different way of accounting for a body of data, and they may perhaps best be regarded as 'models' of the human personality, related to it in the same way as are the models used in the physical sciences to the phenomena that they represent. The model of a molecule of sugar as represented by a chemist is rather different from the picture presented by a nuclear physicist. Yet both models are equally valid, and they work equally well in their respective fields. Science teachers often put across the concept of valency of different elements by regarding the atoms of these elements as being equipped with varying numbers of 'hooks', which are available for making bonds with other elements. Nobody is, of course, suggesting that there really are little hooks on atoms, and even the word 'bonds' is nothing but a model drawn from something that we are fairly familiar with. Any discussion as to whether this model is a 'true theory' is manifestly a waste of time. Similarly, psycho-analysts discuss the development of the child's personality in terms of the three main institutions of the personality – the ego, the super-ego and the id. The ego may be regarded as a reality-based part of the mind which mediates between its two powerful neighbours by the use of devices like repression which are known collectively as defence mechanisms. It is very tempting to ask whether there really is, for instance, such a thing as the ego, and even some of the people who make use of the terms often appear to be according to them some kind of independent reality. But surely this is not the point. The point is, does the use of these terms provide us with a model which, at least in certain contexts, enables us to understand people a bit better, to help their development, and to have some chance of predicting what they will do next? We should not find it at all surprising to meet someone who will adopt whatever model seems most appropriate for the aspect of development under discussion, talking about the ego for, say, some aspects of moral development, and about conditioned reflexes when trying to understand the formation of some habits. It is too easy, however, and perhaps too comfortable, to settle down as the adherent of a particular school of thought. This is a pity because, when it happens, it limits the number of aspects of the subject we are capable of really understanding.

All this is clearer and much more useful if we see it as being applied to an actual case.

We are watching a baby lying in its cot. It moves its arm in the direction of its face, inserts its thumb into its mouth and begins to

106   CHILD DEVELOPMENT

suck. What are we to say about this simple action in terms of
'rival' theories of development?

Personality psychologists – particularly those associated with
the psycho-analytic school of thought – would give an account
of this behaviour at two levels. Firstly, it is related to need reduc-
tion. The child is hungry. Satisfaction of this is associated with
the insertion of something into his mouth, and we have a kind of
substitute incomplete satisfaction of a primary drive. Secondly,
it can be argued that the child wants his mother. His need can be
viewed as going beyond a simple physical want, and as arising
from a deeper need in the field of interpersonal relationships.
Piaget, on the other hand, would see thumb sucking as marking
the accomplishment of a stage of achievement. That the child can
now accurately place his thumb into his mouth with no false tries
is indicative that a certain level of nervous and muscular co-
ordination has been reached, and further developments, not only
in muscular co-ordination, but also to do with the formation of
concepts about such things as space and movement are ultimately
based on experimental behaviour like this, together with a host of
similar examples.

Is there anything contradictory in these two divergent views of
the same action? I think not. Each approach is concerned with a
different aspect of the child's development. There seems to be no
reason why thumb sucking should not be indicative of physical or
emotional needs *and* at the same time a mark of progress in
physical co-ordination.

One final point:

Because of the nature of the task of this book, a great deal of
space has been given to concepts used in child development, and
to developmental theories. But these are not the main point. It is
necessary to have some acquaintance with them, if one is to use
them as tools in further study, but they should never be allowed
to become an end in themselves. The real subject of child development study must always be children.

SUGGESTIONS FOR FURTHER READING

It is obviously impossible to give an exhaustive bibliography of even the most important works in so large a field. Instead, I am suggesting a few titles which may be useful to those who wish to follow up the subject. Preference has been given to books which do not make too great a demand on the reader in terms of technical vocabulary (though most of them are rather more advanced than is the material presented in this book) and to those which are available in paperback form.

1. *General Books on Child Development*
L. J. Stone and J. Church, *Childhood and Adolescence*, Random House, New York, 1957.
P. L. Mussen, *The Psychological Development of the Child*, Prentice-Hall, New Jersey, 1963.
J. A. Hadfield, *Childhood and Adolescence*, Penguin Books, 1962.
C. W. Valentine, *The Normal Child*, Penguin Books, 1946.
J. Bowlby, *Child Care and the Growth of Love,* Penguin Books, 1953.

2. *Books on Heredity*
Ashley Montague, *Human Heredity*, Mentor Books, 1960.
T. Dobzhansy, *Mankind Evolving*, Yale University Press, 1962.
This book deals with rather more than the mechanisms of inheritance, but in the relevant chapters these are explained with great clarity.

3. *Books dealing with the three theories of development described in Part II.*

(a) Jean Piaget has written a formidable number of books on various aspects of the child's conceptual development. Before looking at these, however, it might be as well to read one of the introductory books now available, such as:

M. Brearley and E. Hitchfield, *A Teacher's Guide to Reading Piaget*, Routledge, 1966.

N. Isaacs, *The Growth of Understanding in Young Children*, Ward Lock, 1961.

(b) Erikson, too, has a considerable publication list, but one of his most important books is now available as a paperback, and this should not present too great a difficulty to the general reader. This is:

Erik H. Erikson, *Childhood and Society*, Penguin Books, 1965.

(c) Ausubel's work is likely to present difficulties to the non-specialist. Commentaries are not available, nor is there a paper-back edition. Nevertheless, this work well repays the attention of those who wish to specialize in this area.

D. P. Ausubel, *Theory and Problems of Child Development*, Grune & Stratton, N.J., 1958.

Theory and Problems or Adolescent Development, Grune & Stratton, N.J., 1954.

4. Readers who wish to take up the comments on the nature of the average and the normal distribution in Chapter V may like to look at:

M. J. Moroney, *Facts from Figures*, Penguin Books, 1951.

Although this book moves on in its later chapters to deal with some very advanced statistics, the earlier chapters are readily comprehensible and entertaining.

Index